Sep. 8, 2010

How to
SURVIVE
Your
PhD

The Insider's Guide to
AVOIDING MISTAKES,
CHOOSING THE
RIGHT PROGRAM,
WORKING WITH
PROFESSORS,
and JUST HOW A PERSON
ACTUALLY WRITES A
200-PAGE
PAPER

Jason R. Karp, PhD

SOURCEBOOKS, INC.®

Published by Sourcebooks, Inc.
P.O. Box 4410, Naperville, Illinois 60567-4410
(630) 961-3900
Fax: (630) 961-2168
www.sourcebooks.com

Library of Congress Cataloging-in-Publication Data

Karp, Jason.
 How to survive your PhD : the insider's guide to avoiding mistakes, choosing the right program, working with professors, and just how a person actually writes a 200-page paper / by Jason Karp.
  p. cm.
 1. Doctor of philosophy degree. I. Title.
LB2386.K37 2009
378.2'4--dc22

2009030718

Printed and bound in the United States of America.
VP 10 9 8 7 6 5 4 3 2 1

Contents

Preface

Throughout my work on my PhD, I always told people that I was the least academic doctoral student they'd ever meet. My academic advisor, of course, wished that wasn't the case.

I told people that partly because it was true and partly because I didn't want people (cute female undergraduates) to think I was a nerd. Truth be told, most doctoral students *are* nerds. I should know—after thirteen years of multiple university educations, including a year of classes in medical school, I've been around many of them. So I felt like I needed some way to connect with a student body that was, with each passing year, getting younger than me. If people saw that I was smart and cool…well, let's just say that everyone wants to feel like part of a group. From the very beginning of graduate school, I saw myself as being different from my peers. I had different career aspirations and a different way of looking at things. I didn't see the point of working hard on papers that only a professor would ever read. I didn't believe there was much value in the rush to publish scientific papers in academic journals so that your articles could gather dust on university library bookshelves, their cobwebs only being blown off when some other stressed graduate student needs to reference your esoteric paper for his or her own dissertation. Instead, I wanted a larger audience. If I was going to be a student living in a college town, I'd rather hang on to the college lifestyle as long as I could. Believe me, it helps immensely when you look a decade younger than you really are. In fact, I still get carded at the door when I go out to a bar or a nightclub.

At the outset of my PhD, my career goal was to be an entrepreneur. I wanted to work for myself as a running and fitness coach, writer, and consultant, but I also wanted flexibility, with the option to work in academia if I wanted. While I initially thought it would take four years to complete my degree, it ended up taking seven, giving a whole new meaning to the term "seven-year itch."

Obviously, there were many obstacles to overcome and much waiting to endure while working on my PhD, and naturally, I often questioned whether I was ever going to finish. At times, I felt like Estragon and Vladimir in Samuel Beckett's *Waiting for Godot*. Many told me (or tried to tell me) that a PhD certainly wasn't necessary for my career aspirations. But despite the obstacles and the stress and the sometimes not-so-subtle signs that maybe I wasn't smart enough or worthy enough or savvy enough to earn a PhD, I continued forward, blindly at times, to find ways that I could complete my degree. After all, even the great Albert Einstein attempted multiple times to get a dissertation accepted and eventually receive his doctorate, so busy he was revolutionizing the field of physics and all. However, I didn't have such distractions. "Why am I doing this to myself?" I asked myself countless times. Looking back, perhaps the reason was because I put the PhD degree on such a high pedestal, a pedestal that I wanted to stand on. Although there may always be a good chance of failing, people take risks because the chance of failing makes success taste even sweeter. For me, the truth was that, if I had quit, I would have felt guilty for the rest of my life. So I pushed ahead with the degree, hoping for the best.

This book is the culmination of years of hard work and much frustration that could have been avoided if only I had had someone to give me the advice that I am now trying to give you. That said, you won't hear the advice in this book from professors and others working in academia, nor from any other book on this subject. Sure, people like me can give you advice and help make your path a smoother one; however, the fact is that no one can tell you what your exact experience will be like. That's the reason that I wrote this book, after all.

In *How to Survive Your PhD*, I'll walk you through the entire PhD process and give details about exactly what you'll need to know, details such as how to choose your school and advisor, what demands to expect on your time, where delays can occur and how to deal with them, among many other invaluable tidbits. But even more than great tips and strong advice, this book tries to give you a thorough understanding of the human elements of the PhD process—for example, how to deal with the people to whom you must prove yourself—and hopefully bestow on you the insight I lacked during those years.

To give you a clearer picture of the process and the situations in which you may find yourself, text boxes are included throughout the book that speak to my personal experiences, most of which end with a lesson. But until you experience the PhD process for yourself, it's all theory, not reality. Acknowledging this limitation, it is my sincere hope that this book will help you make the right decisions both before and during your doctoral work, simplifying and facilitating the PhD process for all you future doctors in your respective fields. Follow the advice in this book, and you'll become a doctor a lot sooner and with much less stress.

And at the very least, this book may help to pay off the huge debt I've incurred as a result of spending thirteen years in school, seven years of which were spent on my PhD. So tell all of your friends to buy a copy.

Acknowledgments

It would be an understatement to simply say that there are many people to thank for helping complete a publication like this. Writing the acknowledgments section of a book feels, I assume, much like giving an acceptance speech at the Oscars. Regardless of your sincerity, you're sure to overlook someone who was instrumental to your work. And, much like the Oscars, it is an egregious sin to not thank your mother. So first and foremost, I would like to take this opportunity to thank my mother, Muriel, who, despite her wishes for me to get a real job and a wife and present her with a few grandchildren, has always wanted what is best for me and always supported the decisions I have made in life.

I also want to thank my twin brother, Jack, who unfortunately suffered the brunt of my complaints during the seven years that I worked on my PhD, telling me repeatedly to "suck it up." If it weren't for his sarcastic wit that provided me with laughter when I needed it most, there's no doubt I would have gone nuts. Receiving my PhD and writing this book would not have been as fulfilling without the opportunity to share it with my mother and brother.

I'd also like to thank Cairril Mills for planting the initial seeds for the writing of this book and for her ability to help me see things rationally while I was working on my PhD degree (not to mention for her award-winning brownies); my wonderful agent, Grace Freedson, for helping make this book become a reality; my editor, Peter Lynch, and his colleagues at Sourcebooks; and my doctoral dissertation advisor Dr. Robert Robergs of the University of New Mexico, without whom my PhD degree, and consequently this book, may never have been completed. At a time when I needed a hand to save me from drowning, Rob lent his and lifted me to a height that I never would have been able to reach on my own. I will never be able to thank him enough.

CHAPTER 1

Choices

"Life is the sum of all your choices."
—ALBERT CAMUS

When I was in high school, my electronics teacher had a silly, fortune-cookie saying to remind his students not to touch electrical wires with two hands and risk shock: "One hand in pockey, no get shockey." Like touching wires with both hands, there's a wrong way to do almost everything. For example, going down a park slide head first, throwing a paper airplane at your high school teacher, and not buying your twin brother a birthday present, instead claiming that you forgot his birthday, would all be considered by most as errors in judgment. I'll be the first to admit I don't always make the best decisions; but I've learned a great deal from my mistakes and, hopefully, you can, too.

Life, as we all know, is full of choices. Some choices are big (like where you attend college, who you marry, whether or not you have kids), but some choices are small (like which movie you see, whether you buy a microwave at Target or Walmart, whether you have a grande peppermint mocha Frappuccino or a venti chai latté at Starbucks). Some of the choices we make are good, and some are bad. However, the key to making any choice, especially the more important ones, is information. The more information we have about our options, the better the chance of making good decisions. And when it comes to getting a PhD degree, there are many options and many choices.

CHOOSING THE PhD

Everyone is different, and naturally, people choose to get a PhD for a variety of reasons, including:

- For the pursuit of knowledge
- For the prerequisite to becoming a college professor
- For the love of research
- For future professional opportunities
- For the delay of getting a job
- For status and acclaim
- For fear of "the real world"
- For an ego boost (my favorite reason)

Ego

Ego is such a big part of the PhD that it should be spelled with a capital E. Despite what someone tells you is his or her reason for achieving a doctorate degree, there is always at least some amount of Ego behind it—there are tons of people in academia with big Egos. After all, it's pretty cool to be called "doctor." Let's face it: it makes you feel good.

Did you know that less than 1 percent of the U.S. population has a PhD? According to the Chronicle of Higher Education and National

Science Foundation, 43,354 PhDs were awarded by U.S. schools in 2005 (their most recent data). Of these, 27,974 were awarded in science and engineering disciplines, and 15,380 were awarded in liberal arts and humanities disciplines. In the sciences, 7,406 PhDs were awarded in agricultural science; biological science; computer science; earth, atmospheric, and ocean sciences; and mathematics; 3,647 were awarded in chemistry; physics; astronomy; psychology; and social sciences; and 6,404 were awarded in engineering (e.g., chemical, civil, electrical, mechanical, and other types). Sounds like a lot of PhDs hanging around, but these figures are actually quite small when you consider there are over 300 million people living and working in the United States.

These small numbers are one reason why doctors, whether they've earned PhDs or MDs, hold such a prestigious role in society today. People look up to them. Ego may not be the driving force behind someone's decision to pursue his or her PhD, but it's usually there if you look deep enough.

MY REASONS FOR CHOOSING TO PURSUE A PhD DEGREE:

Before embarking on your journey, you need to know why you are doing this in the first place. Ask yourself right now, before turning past this page of this book, why you are choosing to pursue a PhD degree. Write those reasons in the spaces below. Go ahead. I'll wait.

1. _____

_____

2. _____

_____

3. _____

_____

4. _____

_____

5. _____

_____

Only have a few reasons to list? Only one? Don't worry. You don't need to have many reasons. A single good one is enough. But if that one reason is that you'd rather not get a job, you're headed for trouble. Choosing to attend graduate school solely because you can effectively postpone your entry into the real world is exactly how not to earn your PhD.

On the other hand, choosing to attend graduate school solely because you're driven by your Ego is perfectly fine (despite what others may tell you). Don't confuse Ego with being egocentric. By definition, Ego is a division of the psyche that refers to a sense of self and serves as the conscious mediator between the self and reality, whereas egocentric means the quality of being selfish and self-centered. There have been many successful people who have accomplished many great things in their lifetimes because they were driven by their Egos, never being egocentric. There's absolutely nothing wrong with pursuing a PhD because you want to develop or heighten your sense of self; that is, of course, as long as you don't allow the degree to fully define you as a person and take over your whole life.

Don't enter a PhD program thinking that it will be your ticket to some cushy college professor job with three to four months off every summer. Sure, it could happen, but that's not what a PhD really means. It's about learning, about working your tail off, about striving for excellence, about the process of becoming a scholar. And, when it's all done, for the honor of being called "Doctor" with all of its privileges and responsibilities.

WHY CHOOSE THE PhD PATH?

I chose to join a PhD program for a few reasons, but mainly because I wanted to become an entrepreneur and I wanted to acquire a level of freedom and independence that I thought I would not have been able to acquire without the degree. I love learning, and I believe that knowledge is power, but what started as a quest for knowledge unfortunately turned into a means to an end, a change that started at the end of my fifth year. As an entrepreneur, I believed the degree would open doors for me that may not have been otherwise opened. The chance to write and publish books, obtain high-paying consulting jobs, invitations to speak in front of others, all would have been harder to obtain without the PhD punctuating my name. But first and foremost, pursuing my PhD was about developing a higher level of understanding and thinking so that I could finally play with the "big boys" for the rest of my career, distinguish myself from other entrepreneurs in my field, and also (obviously) so that I could offer the best service to those who hired me. Envisioning my future, whatever I decided to do afterward, having already gone through that rigorous academic process would allow me to operate on a higher level; and it can (and will) do the same for you as well.

Finances

From a purely financial perspective, the choice to pursue a PhD is rather stupid. Unlike your MD counterpart, who will likely command a six-figure salary after completing his or her residency, you sink far into debt with no guaranteed way to pay back your student loans when you graduate. While your high school and college friends are making lots of money, living the American dream, and saving for their retirement, you may find yourself barely scraping by in your studio or one-bedroom apartment, sleeping on a futon and eating TV dinners, pasta, and macaroni and cheese for years, especially if you're single. If you're a married doctoral student, you'll likely have it a bit easier, unless of course your spouse is also a doctoral student. When you finally graduate, you may have to postpone buying a house with that white picket fence because of your monthly student loan payments that ominously stare at you from the coffee table like an appointment notice from the dentist. When you're out in the real world, the people you associate with will probably have houses with real wood furniture and marble islands in their kitchens and expensive cars in their driveways.

Unlike the more highly respected MDs with their six-figure salaries, most PhDs must settle for underpaid faculty positions. In my discipline of exercise physiology, as in many science-related disciplines, the starting salary when I graduated in 2007 was between $45,000 and $50,000 per year. Everyone I knew who got tenure-track faculty positions was making that salary range, too. This salary is rather insulting when you consider the amount of time, effort, and money spent on becoming an expert in your discipline and obtaining a level of education that fewer than 1 percent of the population ever achieve.

While it's possible in disciplines like engineering, statistics, and psychology to get a well-paying job outside of academia, it's not the norm for PhD graduates in most disciplines. For example, according to the National Research Council, more than 95 percent of the approximately 46,000 graduates with PhDs in the humanities who are employed full-time are faculty members (assistant, associate, and full professors) at universities, receiving lower-than-expected salaries. My former doctoral advisor had been working for over twenty years at the same university before he finally received a six-figure salary.

If, however, money is not your driving factor (and your parents have left you boatloads of money in their wills), earning a PhD can have its own intrinsic reward. Whatever your reasons for pursuing your doctoral degree, make sure the PhD is what you really, really want, because the process of obtaining it will consume your life for years.

Now, assuming you've already made the choice to pursue a PhD in your chosen field, which is likely why you are reading this book in the first place, your next important decision is where to pursue your doctorate.

CHOOSING YOUR SCHOOL: LOCATION, LOCATION, LOCATION

When choosing your school, it's important to remember why you are attending. Sure, it would be nice to study for exams underneath a palm tree or write your dissertation from your balcony while looking at the beautiful city skyline; but choosing your school solely on its location is yet another example of how not to successfully earn your PhD.

Where you pursue your PhD is extremely important. To a large extent, your choice of school will dictate your educational experience and the perspective you'll gain in your discipline of study. Your decision will also help build your reputation among other scholars, most of whom know where the strong programs are located and the people working in them. However, you also want to be happy where you live because, simply put, not being happy makes you unhappy. And being unhappy only contributes to the negative feelings of bitterness, misery, depression, and apathy, none of which are good feelings to possess when you're trying to ace difficult classes or work on your dissertation.

Many students first choose schools in their home states. While this is especially true at the undergraduate level, it is less so at the graduate level. Close proximity to family and the cost of tuition are factors that influence the decisions of most students. I've also noticed that many undergraduates remain at the same school for their graduate education, either for the same reasons as location and cost or perhaps because it's simply easier to stay where they have lived for years rather than to move somewhere unfamiliar. Let's face it—picking up and moving to a new state where you don't know anyone else, finding a place to live, starting at a new school, and adopting a new routine can all seem a bit daunting.

While these are valid concerns, don't let them limit your opportunities. Getting your graduate degree from the same university as your undergraduate degree will only give you one perspective of your discipline and show future employers that you aren't willing to make a change or think outside the box. I know a few people who received all three of their degrees—their bachelor's, their master's, as well as their doctorate—from the same university. Obviously, this doesn't look especially good to potential employers and certainly does not help to open your mind. Think bigger. To rub elbows with the best, sometimes you have to travel to where the best are.

When choosing your school, the location should only be a factor if you really believe, after visiting, that you will be miserable living there. Essentially, you will have to decide if going to a particular school is worth living in a place where you don't want to live. Never choose a school without first visiting. Tour the campus. Walk around the town or city. Get as good of a feeling for the place and atmosphere as you can. Ask other grad students to lunch, during which time you can ask questions. Don't forget to visit the library, too, because you will undoubtedly spend a great deal of time there. Make sure to do all these things at each school you are considering.

When it's time to make a choice, go with your gut. A good school is one thing, but personal happiness with your surroundings is quite another. Ideally, you will have both; but if you can't study in paradise, a plastic palm tree, some pink flamingos in your living room, and a Beach Boys CD on repeat can help you forget that it's 20 degrees outside and snowing. And sticking your head in your freezer can feel invigorating in the middle of summer when it's 90 degrees outside with 70 percent humidity.

PALM TREES

I've always loved palm trees. For me, they represent vacation, sunshine, paradise, a laid-back way of living. Bare trees just seem more stressful to me. They're weathered; they represent cold winters. So why did I choose to attend four schools that donned bare trees for almost half the year? Because, as my logical, education-driven family told me on numerous occasions, "You shouldn't pick a school based on the location." Consequently, there were no palm trees in my education, unless you count the plastic blow-up one that sat on the end table in my apartment. But my absent palm trees were soon replaced by opportunities, some of which I took, some of which I neglected; but that's another story that we'll get to later.

OPPORTUNITY

Unlike what we are usually told, opportunity does not knock only once. Truth is, it knocks many times in our lives, primarily because there are plenty of opportunities and probably because many of us are not listening close enough to recognize opportunity the first time it knocks. How many times have I wrongly convinced myself that the knocks of some of my opportunities sounded like door-to-door salesmen, ignoring them as a result? Take my word for it—there will be plenty of opportunities when you are working on your PhD, opportunities including:

- Working side-by-side with faculty and experts
- Conversing with other graduate students about issues in your discipline

- Taking a wide variety of classes on various subjects
- Teaching undergraduate students about your field
- Becoming involved with research projects
- Presenting your research at academic conferences
- Sharing your research findings with scholarly communities by publishing your work
- Conveying your research findings to the general public
- And many more…

The key to PhD success is the ability to recognize these opportunities when they present themselves. You want to choose a school that will offer you the maximum number of opportunities, one that matches your research interests, too. For example, maybe there's a certain person you admire in your discipline and working with him or her would help you learn what you wouldn't otherwise learn somewhere else. To be the best, you need to rub elbows with the best. Choose a school that will give you the best opportunities to learn and become successful. Then, stay on the lookout for other opportunities so that you can take advantage of them when you arrive on campus.

"THE HIP BONE IS CONNECTED TO THE THIGH BONE"

One of the opportunities I had while working on my PhD was teaching anatomy and physiology courses at a local hospital to people who worked in medical technology. Despite needing the money, I declined that opportunity, mostly because I wanted to remain focused on completing my PhD as quickly as possible. I've never been a good multitasker; I'm more of a serial worker. I like to focus on one thing at a time, see it to completion, and then begin the next project. But sometimes this shortsightedness has cost me. Teaching science-based classes to health care professionals would have looked great on my résumé. Looking back, that was definitely a missed opportunity to grow, both professionally and personally.

COURSEWORK

Most doctoral programs in the United States are course-intensive. For the first two to three years of your PhD degree, you will take a full load of courses each semester. Since each school will have different requirements, find out what courses you will be required to pass before choosing your school. Call the department secretary or your future academic advisor, and ask for a list of required courses. You don't want any surprises once you're enrolled (like finding out you have to spend a whole year taking classes with hotshot medical students who think that MDs are the only real doctors and whose memorization skills are sharper than those of a Broadway actor).

No matter which school you attend, if you're in a scientific discipline, then you will have to take at least a few statistics courses. Statistics are an important part of doing research. Of course, you have to analyze and interpret all of the data you generate. While you may never take statistics if you enter into the liberal arts discipline, many liberal arts programs require proficiency in a foreign language, so you may have to take a few foreign language classes (or prove that you are fluent in a foreign language).

With all of the courses you'll take, it can become extremely difficult to get an A in all of them. After all, these are doctoral-level
classes. If you're getting an A in all of your classes, then you're at a
school that isn't challenging you, you're just brilliant, or, like one
of my professors in the aforementioned medical school classes used
to say, "you're spending too much time studying at the expense
of doing research." Though I only achieved a B in her class, that
professor's lesson is true nonetheless. In the long run, grades do not
matter that much anyway at the doctoral level. Grades just feed
the Ego of exceptional students and frustrate the mediocre ones.
Falling somewhere between exceptional and mediocre, you can
just imagine my confusion. Since everyone coming out of graduate
school has at least a 3.0 grade point average (GPA)—you can't
graduate from most graduate schools without maintaining at least a
B average—the distribution of grades is not very widespread among
students. Whether you graduate with a 4.0 or a 3.0 GPA is not
going to matter to a potential employer. What really matters to the
employer is whether you are qualified, competent, and experienced
enough to successfully work the job. Truth be told, employers tend
to put experience far ahead of education anyway. For example, if
you're planning to apply for faculty positions after you graduate
with your PhD, the department chair or dean of the school who
does the hiring will not care if you graduated with a 4.0 or a 3.4
GPA. He or she will look at your prior teaching and research experience, the number of research publications you have, your letters
of recommendation, your past history in acquiring research grants,
and your overall potential fit within the department. With no full-
time university faculty experience, you can't expect to get a job at
a top school in your discipline in a popular part of the country to
live—even if your transcript shows a 4.0 GPA.

STATISTICS: A NECESSARY EVIL

While I recognize that one must learn statistics in order to complete research, for me, these classes were a necessary evil. Obviously, I didn't care much for stats. So I decided that the best way to make my required statistics courses interesting was to write a book about statistics. The lesson here is simple: when you're required to work on something you don't necessarily want to do, try to make it interesting by taking the class or activity in a different direction.

REPUTATION OF DEPARTMENT

When searching for a school at which you could pursue your PhD, the reputation of the academic department is more important than the reputation of the university itself. Attending Harvard is great, but if Harvard doesn't offer a PhD program in your discipline or if Harvard's academic department of your intended discipline does not have a strong reputation, it makes no sense to enroll there—not to mention the fact that it's too easy to get blinded by all the ivy, some of which I swear is poisonous. Of course, you want to stand on the shoulders of giants who came before you, so it goes to reason that you should want to attend a school where there are some giants in your discipline (or at least people bigger than you). When you eventually apply for a faculty job, it won't be lost on the interviewer that you studied under the Nobel Laureate, Dr. Jason Karp—I don't really have a Nobel Prize, but it sounds good, doesn't it?

Besides the faculty on staff, the volume of quality research coming out of the department and the dissemination of the research at conferences also contributes to a university's and department's reputation. With that in mind, check the activity of the department at the conferences in your discipline. How many abstracts did the department submit last year? How many conference presentations were given by faculty and students from the department? How many research grants does the department receive annually? What were the dissertation topics of recent students? Did those students get postdoc positions after finishing their PhDs? If so, where?

NOBEL BY ASSOCIATION

While visiting schools to decide where to matriculate, I met a student in the final year of his degree who told me that he chose to attend that specific university because his advisor (we'll call him Dr. Nobel) studied under the top person in the discipline (we'll call him Dr. Laureate). If he couldn't study under Dr. Laureate himself, he figured the next best thing would be to study under the person who studied under Dr. Laureate. Not a bad idea. I took that student's advice and also studied under Dr. Nobel. You'll find that you will be influenced by the faculty with whom you work, just like they were influenced by those with whom they worked.

KNOW YOUR RESEARCH INTERESTS

It is vital to spend time thinking about your research interests before applying to schools for your PhD degree. While you'll undoubtedly take lots of classes, the PhD is considered a research degree. As such, the focus of the most reputable PhD programs is preparing their students for careers in research, so you're going to spend a great deal of time engaged in research.

If you don't yet know what exact area of research you want to pursue, or if your interests are not specific or focused enough, then you probably aren't ready for a PhD program. If you want to pursue a doctorate but are not keen on research, there are some other options available, such as an EdD (Doctor of Education), JD (Juris Doctor, or Doctor of Law), PsyD (Doctor of Psychology), or DSc (Doctor of Science). Of course, there's also an MD, but that's another book altogether.

Not only does having merely a fuzzy idea of your research interests sell you poorly to the admissions committees reading your "Statement of Purpose" within your graduate school application, but you can also end up attending a school that isn't necessarily right for you. This doesn't mean you need to know the exact topic of your dissertation before applying. In fact, you shouldn't know that yet. You may not even be given the chance to pick your dissertation topic anyway, as your advisor may advise you on what topic to pursue. If you're in a scientific discipline, you'll likely pursue a dissertation topic that is an extension of the research of those students who came before you as well as one that fits within the research agenda of your advisor and the department. If you're going into a liberal arts or multidisciplinary field, however, then you may have more freedom in choosing your own topic. I've known students in both situations—those who were told exactly what they were going to research and those who were allowed to choose anything they wanted.

Going to graduate school without knowing which specific area of research you want to pursue is yet another example of how not to get your PhD degree. If you know where your interests lie, you can pick an advisor with the same interests you have (see Choosing Your Academic Advisor). Writing your research interests on paper will force you to think about what you want to study and help make your ideas more concrete. Try listing your research interests below, starting with some general areas and then listing specific ones.

MY GENERAL RESEARCH INTERESTS:

1. _____

_____

2. _____

_____

3. _____

_____

4. _____

_____

5. _____

_____

MY SPECIFIC RESEARCH INTERESTS:

1. _____

_____

2. _____

_____

3. _____

_____

4. _____

_____

5. _____

_____

If you can list more than five general or specific research interests, chances are you're not focused enough. As a doctoral student, your research will focus on a very specific area. For example, a general research interest could be "child development," but child development research alone is not specific enough. Listing "factors that influence child development" is still not specific enough, unless you want to spend the rest of your life working on your PhD. What about child development do you want to study? The effect of nutrition on physical maturation? How different types of parenting styles affect behavior? The effect of single-parent homes compared to dual-parent homes on the development of social skills? Another general research interest could be "psychology," and then your specific interests could include the factors influencing deviant behavior among high school students, the effects of serotonin on mood in clinically depressed patients, or the various factors that influence memory. Of course, your dissertation will inevitably become even more specific than these issues as you learn. Ask yourself what you are most interested in studying. More importantly, what excites you?

USING YOUR EXPERIENCES TO CREATE A NICHE

It wasn't long after participating in my first track meet in junior high that I became interested in human motion. There was something exciting about running faster than the guy in the lane next to you, something intriguing about how it was done. Over time, I slowly become interested in the science of sports and exercise. Even at a young age, I knew it was something I wanted to pursue as a career. This passion brought me to places I probably never would have gone otherwise, including a small, rural college town in Pennsylvania named State College, an Olympic city in Canada, a railroad and limestone town in southern Indiana, and the high desert of Albuquerque, New Mexico.

When I started my PhD, I knew I was interested in endurance athletic performance, specifically in runners. Within that large topic, I was most interested in muscle glycogen resynthesis, central and peripheral limitations to maximal oxygen consumption, cardiovascular physiology, the effects of training on carbohydrate and fat metabolism, and the metabolic causes of muscle fatigue. For my dissertation, I researched the coordination between breathing and stride rate in highly trained distance runners running at different speeds to study how this coordination manifested itself and hopefully determine whether or not there was an aerobic advantage to coordinating the breathing and stride rhythms while running.

CHOOSING YOUR ACADEMIC ADVISOR

The relationship between doctoral student and academic advisor is a unique one. There's questioning, challenging, commanding, learning, joking, yielding, yelling—and that's just the first week of school. If you take the time to make the right choice, the relationship you forge with your advisor can become very rewarding. If you don't make the right choice, the relationship can become very frustrating, very quickly. In short, who you choose as your doctoral advisor will make or break your PhD experience.

In my discipline, as in many others, there is a wide array of things to study, from limitations of oxygen consumption in elite endurance athletes to the mechanisms of the blood pressure–lowering effect of exercise in sedentary people to the contractile properties of single muscle fibers biopsied from an animal. That's why it's extremely important to choose an academic advisor whose research interests match your own.

Indeed, one of the key things that will help direct your choice of academic advisors is what his or her line of research includes. That's the reason it's so important to know your own research interests first. If you're interested in studying the effects of strength training on bone mineral density in postmenopausal women, why would you ever enroll in a school where the professors are studying insulin–mediated glucose utilization in diabetic rats? In scientific disciplines, finding a research match with an advisor is usually more important than the reputation of the department or the university. In humanities disciplines, this is not always the case, as the department may be more important than working with any one person. In either case, find out how actively your advisor is involved in research. How many publications has he or she had in the last three years? This will give you an idea of your potential advisor's productivity and his or her ability to help you get published yourself.

After you have pared down your choice to a few potential advisors by familiarizing yourself with their work, call or email them to introduce yourself and discuss the potential of working with them. Tell each of them about yourself, your background, your professional goals, and your interest in working with them. To a certain extent, your status as a new PhD graduate will be based on the reputation of your advisor even more so than on the reputation of the department from which you graduated. For the rest of your career, people will refer to you as "one of Dr. Nobel's students," so try to pick someone who has some clout.

Your Advisor's Work Ethic

Aside from having similar research interests, you should know the work ethic of your potential advisors. Are they good at getting things accomplished, or are they procrastinators? Check out their offices—are they messy with cluttered desks, or are they organized? If any of your potential advisors have papers scattered all over the desk and floor, turn around, walk out of the office, and go find another advisor. If you don't, your dissertation proposal will soon be one of the scattered papers mixed in with the rest. Before you dismiss a cluttered desk as being trivial, trust me, the personality hidden behind it is immensely important when you are trying to publish your research or finish your dissertation. You don't want your advisor misplacing the scholarly work that you've worked so hard to produce. Waiting months for your advisor to read your manuscripts and provide feedback just so you can revise and submit them for publication is another example of how not to get your PhD.

One of the reasons that your chosen advisor may seem incredibly busy is that he or she has a number of students to advise, which I myself have been told more than once. Find out how many doctoral and master's students your advisor currently advises and how many more will enter the program the same time as you. You want your advisor to attend to your needs, and he or she won't be able to do that if he or she is juggling the needs of ten or more other students. Bear in mind that most reputable graduate programs have three to five doctoral students (plus a few master's degree students) per advisor at any one time.

Your Advisor's Philosophy

Since the PhD, after all, stands for Doctor of Philosophy (or Piled Higher and Deeper, as some cynics will tell you), find out what your advisor's philosophy is. This may be the most important thing you find out about your advisor, as it can make or break your working relationship. Here are some questions you should ask:

- How do you see your role as an advisor?
- How much control do you keep, and how much do you give to your students? If you're someone who likes to be in control, you want an advisor who gives a lot of control to his or her students. Conversely, if you don't like to be in control, you don't want an advisor who gives control to his or her students since that may be too overwhelming for you. On the other hand, if you and your advisor both prefer to be in control, then that may pose a serious problem.
- Do you micromanage your students or do you leave them alone to do their own work? Again, the answer to this question is important in relation to how you like to work. If you're independent and like to work on your own, you want an

advisor who doesn't micromanage his or her students. On the other hand, if you're not good at setting and meeting deadlines for yourself, you tend to procrastinate, or you're a tad disorganized, you may want someone to micromanage you and make sure you get the work done on time.

- Do you allow your students to initiate and voice their own research ideas, or do you start your students with an idea and let them make it their own?

- If I come up with an idea, who retains the intellectual property? This question may sound like putting the cart before the horse, especially since you haven't even begun your degree yet, but it's important to know where your advisor stands on this issue and what the department's or university's policy is because you don't want problems later. Many advisors wrongly think that they own their students' research, especially in scientific disciplines.

- Where do you stand on authorship for publications? This is important, primarily because being the first author on a published article will help foster your professional development. Many advisors allow their students to be the first author, but others, especially if the idea is theirs, will want to be first author themselves.

- How do you measure your students' success? If your advisor isn't clear about his or her methods for evaluating achievement, you'll have no benchmark by which to judge your own progress. Most advisors want to see certain things or competencies from their students. Find out what those things are from the very beginning.

- How much time do you devote to giving feedback? You want an advisor who actively offers feedback on a regular basis because that shows he or she is committed to the development and success of the students.

- Do you set deadlines for your students and for yourself? Given the open-ended nature of the PhD program, you will definitely need mutually agreeable deadlines.

If you are planning to visit the school before making a decision (and I strongly suggest you do), ask your advisor to go to lunch and get as many answers to the above questions as you can. This meeting will also give you the opportunity to catch a glimpse of his or her personality. There are a lot of big Egos in academia, and many of the potential problems that can arise between students and advisors can be traced back to the size of the Egos involved (from both the advisor and the student). In my experience, I've found this particularly true among scientists. Many scientists seem to think that they have the answers to everything and that they operate on a higher level than the general public.

Seek Information from Others

While you, as the student, must understand that the time you spend working on your PhD is much like an apprenticeship, with certain things, such as the specific topic of your dissertation and submitting manuscripts for publication, deferring to the discretion of your advisor, your advisor must understand that he or she is obligated to usher you through the degree process in a timely manner. If your advisor does not cooperate and this lack of cooperation delays your progress or retards your professional development, you have the right to move forward by seeking help from other faculty members and even choosing a different advisor.

The best way to learn about your potential advisor is to talk to some of the said advisor's current students. During your campus visit, invite some of the other doctoral students to lunch. Over your turkey sandwich and mocha, drill them with questions and ask them for honest answers. After all, you need to hear both the good and the bad points about the department and your future advisor. More often than not, students will be hesitant to say anything negative since they usually feel that they should be diplomatic and loyal to their advisor. But you're sitting on an important decision, so you need to know everything you can.

Sometimes, despite the best intentions, the advisor–student relationship may not work. Mine didn't. Not all relationships do. After all, people are people. Changing advisors can be a delicate matter, but sometimes necessary. If this situation does arise, talk to your advisor first about your interest in working with someone else. Above all, be civil, and respect their position.

THE "PHILOSOPHY" IN DOCTOR OF PHILOSOPHY

My doctoral advisor's philosophy was simple: "You get done when you get done." In fact, that was one of his infamous lines. Five years into my degree, I still had no indication as to when the degree would be completed. When I asked for a date to shoot for, he would just repeat his trademark line.

My doctoral advisor had one of the largest Egos that I have ever come across, and I believe it was the root of the controlling nature he had with his students. Looking back, I made the mistake of not finding out about my doctoral advisor's personality and his professional philosophy as it pertained to the degree process, the manuscript submission and publication process, and getting things accomplished; and thus, it was a rocky road all the way, ending with me changing advisors to one at a different university and moving across the country to complete my dissertation.

Much of the conflict between me and my former advisor could be traced to the fundamental difference with which we approached the degree. My approach was to move forward continuously toward specific goals that lead to degree completion within a set time period. My advisor's approach, however, was to move forward on a timeline that was not articulated to me. When asked, he would not agree to set deadlines or outline timelines with me. Instead, he would hide behind the veil of being busy. In circumstances in which deadlines existed, things were done at the last minute, right before the deadline. He never saw the timeline issue as a problem, which was something I had great difficulty understanding, and led to much disappointment working with him. It got to the point where I felt that I could no longer talk to my advisor about my frustrations and get him to see things from my point of view. I couldn't seem to get him to understand the urgency with which I wanted to complete my degree. So I took a deep breath, composed a long letter detailing the issues between us, and went over his head with the letter to the department chair and the associate dean. These actions, as I predicted in the letter itself, ultimately led to me seeking a different advisor. In hindsight, had I known what to look for and had I gotten honest answers from former and current students, I would never have chosen my particular advisor in the first place, and

I would have saved myself from a lot of unnecessary stress. Looking back, I think I learned more from that advisor in terms of what not to do rather than what actually to do, especially concerning understanding the student's needs.

With my dissertation advisor, I had the exact opposite problem. Instead of not agreeing to set a timeline with me, he would always say that this or that should be done by a certain date. "You'll be done before you know it," he said. Sometimes, the date would come, and I wouldn't be finished. For example, although my advisor said my data collection would be done in three weeks, it took over six months to collect and record all the data for my dissertation. While I appreciated my advisor's interest in helping me complete my dissertation, his "best intentions" approach led to false hopes and inevitable multiple disappointments. Things always take longer than what you think at the outset. You need an advisor who will be accountable and willing to set a firm timeline with you, but one who will also be honest with you and himself about how long things will take.

The difference between my two advisors was like night and day. My dissertation advisor, who completed his own PhD in just three years, worked side-by-side with his students, with a real interest in helping them complete their degrees. When I once asked him, "How did you complete your PhD in three years?" he replied, "My advisor pushed me." It was then that I fully realized how important the decision of choosing an advisor truly is. He saw his role on my dissertation research as a collaborator rather than as a dictator who makes demands from his ivory tower. My former advisor basically left his students to figure things out on their own, citing "that's part of earning a PhD." After a few years, though, I began to realize that that wasn't the truth, that he was just hiding behind that philosophy. The truth was that he was too busy (or made himself too busy) to get his hands dirty. The nearly five years I spent with him as my advisor, I don't recall ever seeing him actually do any research in the lab. My dissertation advisor, by contrast, was always in the lab.

CHOOSING YOUR COMMITTEE

The doctoral committee is the jury of the PhD degree. Ultimately, it will be up to its members whether or not you receive your PhD. You will spend countless hours and many late nights trying to convince them, through your preparation, your reasoning, and your writing, that you are worthy of joining their exclusive fraternity. And when you think you have finally figured it all out, they will tell you that you haven't. So what do you do? You stack the deck in your favor.

Just like an employer who conducts interviews to hire who he or she hopes to be the right person for the job, you should "interview" faculty members to serve on your committee. You, too, want the right people for the right job. Ask potential committee members what they expect to see from a student. Ask them how you can show them what it is they want to see from your research. Find out what specific roles each one will play in helping you reach your goal. Maybe most importantly, find out if they like you.

You will actually have two committees while you work on your PhD—a comprehensive or qualifying exam committee and a dissertation research committee (see Chapter 5 for information on the qualifying exam; see Chapter 6 for information on the dissertation). Sometimes, the members of the two committees are the same; other times, they are not. Much of this organization depends on how good of a job you did choosing the exam committee. Choosing (or being forced to choose) someone for the dissertation research committee who had previously failed you during the qualifying exam is another way to neglect earning your PhD degree.

While the purpose of the exam committee is just for that—your exam—the purpose of the dissertation committee is entirely different. The dissertation committee is there to give you feedback and help sculpt your dissertation. As such, its members should be invested and involved in your research process.

I found this out a bit late in my graduate career, as my advisor would not let me share my dissertation proposal with my committee until after he had read my pages and went through the revision process with me. I suppose he expected that I would be handing my committee members a finished product; but the process of obtaining a PhD is not a back-and-forth affair with you and your advisor alone indefinitely. It's supposed to involve the other members of your committee—they are there to protect the student and move things along, after all.

Your committee is typically composed of two to four members (sometimes more) from your academic department and one member from a different department (called the external member). The external member on the exam committee should (and usually must) represent an area that you have studied, such as a professor you had for a class outside of your department or a representative of your minor discipline of study. In regards to the dissertation committee, the external member is there to make sure the process is carried out fairly. While helpful, it is not necessary that the external member on the dissertation committee possess extensive knowledge of your research topic. You already have people within your department to address your research details and conclusions.

When you choose your exam and dissertation committees, there are a number of things to keep in mind. While there may be people both within and outside your department who you want to include on your committee—either because of their stature or because of what you believe they can contribute to your research—remember that the more people you have on your committee, the more people from whom you have to field questions and the more people you have to satisfy. To ensure your dissertation defense goes smoothly, it's best to have the minimum number of people required on your committee. There's no reason to make things harder on yourself by having more people present to challenge you and revising your dissertation multiple times to satisfy everyone. Remember, a subjective degree like a PhD means you will get many different opinions. The more people you have on your committee, the more opinions with which you're going to have to deal.

Since the committee, along with your advisor, can make or break your PhD experience, you want to choose people who will go out of their way to help you. Just like with choosing your advisor, you want to choose people who practice the same philosophy and the same work ethic as you. You also want to choose people who have a vested interest in your research and will likely work well together. Newer faculty members, who have not yet received tenure, are great choices for committees because they tend to be more energetic and often feel they have something to prove to earn the respect of their colleagues (and eventually obtain tenure). As a result, these professors will be interested in helping you because they will also be helping themselves. Since they are the poster boys and girls of the "publish or perish" adage often heard in academia, they need you as much you need them.

There are also people you want to avoid including on your committee. For example, don't choose a dean to be on your committee. Deans are busy people, probably too busy to properly participate in your dissertation defense. In addition to their involvement with students, bear in mind that they have a number of administrative responsibilities, responsibilities that will likely take their time away from you and your degree. I ended up having two deans on my dissertation committee, and I often found myself extremely low on their priority list. I had to constantly remind them about reading my dissertation proposal, signing and submitting paperwork to the graduate school, and other administrative tasks, reminders that they probably didn't like receiving any more than I liked giving; but sometimes it was the only way to keep them on task. Having too many important people on your committee who don't have time for you is yet another example of how not to successfully earn your PhD.

You also don't want "old fogies" on your committee. Old fogies—professors who are stuck to old ways—tend to be sticklers, conformists, and traditionalists, and therefore, more critical of your work. In other words, they're old school. I had one old fogy (one of the deans) on my committee, and she was as old school as they came. She even criticized where I placed the page numbers in my dissertation! Old fogies want things done, even written, in a certain way, the way to which they are accustomed, the way tradition dictates. They've been around the block more times than you can count, and that experience allows them greater insight. While this can be helpful at times and could help make the final draft of your dissertation even better, it can also cause more headaches for you as you revise your dissertation for the fifth time. It's better to include at least one or two younger, hipper committee members who don't care about page numbers and don't have the years of experience (both in doing research and sitting on students' committees) to be critical to the point of exasperation. After all, it's just a dissertation. It's not the Constitution or the Declaration of Independence, for crying out loud!

Not only should your committee members like you as a person and student, but they should like each other as well. In other words, you don't want sworn enemies on your committee. It's always possible that some animosity or conflict between committee members get inadvertently redirected at you. Remember, academia is full of big Egos, and sometimes those Egos clash with one another. It's hard enough to get four or five people to agree on anything, much less on the details of your dissertation. Some people will want something done or said one way, while others will want it done or said another way altogether. Trying to please everyone can be a big challenge and will only serve to delay your progress. But if all of your committee members share similar opinions and prefer things done the same way, then that spirit of cooperation will obviously make things progress smoother for you.

On a personal note, there was a professor in the physiology department who taught two of my medical physiology classes, one who I definitely wanted on my dissertation committee. We had some things in common—we were both competitive runners and had engaged in similar research topics—but as it turned out, this professor was a graduate student peer of my advisor back in the day, and the two had somewhat of a bad history. Although I liked this professor and I believed he liked me, it was probably best not to have him on my committee, especially since such an encounter may have caused a prickly situation, myself awkwardly caught in the middle.

Furthermore, you don't want too many people on your committee with too much knowledge of your research area. This may sound counterintuitive, but too many experts huddled in a single room can seriously complicate matters. It will always be an uphill battle to satisfy these many experts. They will undoubtedly want you to change this or change that to get the perfect results. Essentially, too many cooks spoil the pot, and consequently, too many experts spoil the research. You want to be the head chef on your research and perhaps know more about your specific research than your committee members do.

When you finally have the right committee assembled, seek and utilize the advice of its members. Actively involve them in your process. At the same time, remember that the committee has the power to award or deny you your degree. Sucking up can go a long way, especially when you appeal to their larger-than-life Egos. Professors like to hear how great their research is, how great their insights are. Tell them how much you value their opinions. Say things like: "That's brilliant, Dr. Nobel. I never thought of it that way" and "I'm really excited about working with you on this project, Dr. Laureate. I think you offer a lot of great advice." You may not feel 100 percent comfortable sucking up to your committee members, but a little schmoozing can go a long way. While you don't have to brown nose or gush compliments on every occasion, your committee members are people first, with the same tendencies as other people. The more they like you and the more favorable their opinion of you, the more likely they will vote in your favor when it's time for your qualifying exams and dissertation defense.

WHO'S ON FIRST?

My dissertation committee turned out to be reminiscent of Abbott and Costello's sketch comedy, "Who's on First." After I changed advisors, my dissertation committee was composed of my dissertation advisor at a different university and three other members at the university I left—the one from which I would earn my degree. Although it was better for my mental health to leave the university and the advisor with whom I had experienced so much trouble, it also made it difficult to communicate with my committee members since they lived halfway across the country. Most of my communication took place through email, and because they didn't see me, they tended to forget about me. As the saying goes, "Out of sight, out of mind." Of course, I felt that being near my dissertation advisor, whom I trusted, was more important than being near the rest of my committee, but it sure made for a unique experience.

TRANSFERRING SCHOOLS

While working on your PhD degree, there will inevitably be times when things don't go according to plan. But how you deal with your emotions during those times will make all the difference on your outlook and your state of mind. Don't think you have to jump ship just because the waters are rough.

Although transferring schools is much more common among undergraduates than doctoral students, you may be tempted to seek out other opportunities, especially when things are not going as well as you had hoped. But don't transfer schools unless the circumstances are dire. I made this mistake, and it cost me a year (if not more) from my degree.

If you transfer schools, you'll definitely waste some time, which is a valuable commodity when you are trying to earn your PhD as efficiently and effectively as possible. Since every school has different requirements, you can bet that at least some of your credits will not transfer. Likely, there will also be some redundancy between the classes you took at one school and the classes you will take at the other school. I came out of my degree with more biochemistry and statistics knowledge than I care to remember (or will ever use). Even if you ignore all the advice in this chapter and end up at the wrong school, you might do better to stay where you are and get the degree. Despite what you may believe at the time, the grass is not always greener on the other side—unless, of course, you follow my lead and move from New Mexico to Indiana, which does, technically, have greener grass.

When I transferred schools, I thought I was headed for a better opportunity, and thinking that I would still graduate in four years was naïve at best. I left a 4.0 grade point average, a beautiful girlfriend, and a chance to run in the clean, dry air of altitude for what I believed to be greener pastures. Ironically, I ended up moving back to New Mexico to complete my dissertation under my original advisor at the university where I started. Despite the extra time and stress it cost me, the one saving grace was that I believed (and still do believe) that I became a better scientist and a better scholar for having initially transferred schools. The unanswered question is whether my travels were worth the burden.

DO YOU HAVE THE TIME?

Speaking of time, to say that most doctoral programs are very time consuming would be a huge understatement. Before I began my PhD program, I (perhaps naïvely) thought the degree would take only four years. After all, that's usually the way it's advertised by universities. I also knew many students who finished their PhDs in four years or less, so I had many reasons to believe that I, too, would complete mine in that same amount of time. Inexperienced as I was, it never occurred to me that the degree could take much longer, not until after I was already neck deep in the process.

That said, earning a PhD can still take four years or less, provided you have some things working in your favor, namely:

- A list of all required courses, so you know exactly which courses you are required to take and when they must be completed.
- You don't procrastinate when it comes to completing your work, despite the absence of deadlines. I personally knew a doctoral student in anthropology who admitted she watched too much television during the day instead of writing her dissertation.
- An advisor and committee that don't procrastinate in reading your work, providing feedback, and scheduling meetings on time.
- You know the exact topic of your dissertation while you're still taking classes and can begin work on your dissertation proposal.
- No delays from your university's Institutional Review Board to approve your research, but remember that you won't have to worry about this delay if you are not doing research that involves human subjects or animals.
- Cooperation from human subjects for your research. More often than not, researchers are always at the mercy of their subjects.

- You pass your qualifying exam, proposal defense, and dissertation defense on the first try.
- A healthy amount of time spent revising your proposal and dissertation.
- Having quick access to journals, other scholarly materials, and sources (human and otherwise) that you need to write your dissertation.

Since any or all of these things can go awry—and many of them will—don't assume that you'll be done in four years. In fact, many people who begin doctoral programs drop out for one reason or another after admission.

Because of its long-term nature, you had better find out what you're getting yourself into first and assess whether or not you can make the kind of commitment required for a doctoral program. Ask yourself, do you really want to spend more years in school while your friends are out in the real world gaining valuable experience? Do you want to spend more years without a stable income, living in a one-bedroom apartment or sharing a house with five other people, eating macaroni and cheese for dinner? If you pursue your PhD when you're still young and in school, you may lag behind your college friends in job experience and life stability for up to ten years as you graduate. Think about this for a moment. Now ask yourself, "Do I still want to pursue a PhD?"

Whether you're married or have children are also important considerations, especially because you don't want to sacrifice the time you could otherwise spend with your family. Fortunately, despite my mother's constant reminders of her wish for me to get a wife and present her with grandchildren, I was not married while working on my PhD; but I knew a number of people who were married and had children, and I always wondered how they were able to balance their families with their degrees. I'm not sure if I could have lived that life and graduated. Something will always be sacrificed and perhaps neglected as you pursue your degree.

As I've mentioned previously, be sure to collect all the information you can before choosing a school. Find out the average number and range of years it takes students in the department to complete their degrees. Ask the department secretary for a list of your advisor's current students and a list of students who graduated from the department (and under your advisor) in the last ten years. How long have the current students been working on their degrees? For the ones who have already graduated, find out when they began and when they finished their degrees. How many of them completed their schooling within four years? Five years into my PhD program, I realized that only one of my advisor's current students had graduated while I was there, and none of his recently graduated students had completed their degrees within four years. There was even a guy in my department who needed twelve years to finally earn his PhD! This should have set off an alarm or sent up a red flag right away.

Remember, a PhD is a huge time, energy, and financial investment on your part. The longer it takes to complete your degree, the more money it will cost you. Don't forget, no one is going to pay back your student loans for you, after all. After I graduated, I once sent my monthly student loan bill to the members of my committee to see if they would indeed pay for my student loans, but of course they never did, despite the postage-paid envelope I included.

Unlike many bachelor's and master's degrees that are based entirely on coursework, a PhD is more open-ended; however, this very open-ended nature can include great potential for disaster. You don't necessarily graduate when your last final exam is finished in your last course—if it were only that easy! Even other doctoral degrees, like medicine and law, have students who move through their programs together on set schedules and graduate with their classmates. PhD students, on the other hand, don't have a class with which to graduate, so it's important to get an idea of how long your program will take to complete. While the process you go through to earn a PhD is important, you also don't want things to drag on and delay your entry into the real world any longer than you must.

Unless you do, that is. Some people, I found out after starting work on my degree, really don't care how long the program takes, because the longer it takes, the more you can delay getting a real job. School, after all, can be an escape from the real world. It's safe and comfortable. I admit, I would much rather be in school than have a nine-to-five job. But, as I stated at the beginning of this book, you should not pursue a PhD for the sole purpose of delaying your entry into the real world. If you're one of those people who don't care if it takes six, seven, eight, or even more years to complete your PhD, you may save yourself the potential stress that accompanies most students' sense of urgency, but you should also ask yourself why you don't care how long your program takes to complete.

PATIENCE

If someone were to ask me to pick one word to describe my PhD experience, the word would have to be "patience." My lack of patience led to a lot of self-inflicted, unnecessary stress. As a type A, achievement-oriented person, I hated waiting for others, watching wasted days pass on the calendar. Unless you're extremely lucky in securing an advisor and committee who cater to your needs, you're on top of everything you do, and they return all of your work quickly (which rarely happens), expect a great deal of waiting when working on your PhD. And waiting. And waiting. You'll notice that no one will have the sense of urgency that you have. All of your committee members already have their doctorate degrees, and time seems to have clouded their memories of working on their degrees.

Long story short, you're going to need a lot of patience. Academia moves slowly. Be prepared to wait for your advisor to read your research manuscripts that you intend to submit for publication, for your advisor to read your dissertation proposal, for your committee members to read your proposal, for your advisor to read your dissertation, for your committee members to read your dissertation, for your committee members to tell you when they're available so that you can schedule your proposal and dissertation defenses—you'd be surprised how hard and long it takes to get four or five people to agree on a specific date and time to meet—and if you're in a scientific discipline, for your university's Institutional Review Board to approve your research—honestly, while integral to the research process and extremely important to protecting the rights of human subjects, the IRB can be a huge pain in the ass. And then, of course, be prepared to wait to hear about grants and scholarships, not to mention the waiting involved to hear back from journal reviewers and editors.

Undoubtedly, each of these steps include more periods of waiting than actual work, as you'll likely have to make revisions on all your work and resubmit to others to read over again. The major reason why there's so much waiting is because advisors and committee members are busy people and they don't have the same deadlines for finishing their work other than those that are self-imposed. Unlike the "fit for purpose" attitude of business, where things happen fast but not necessarily of the best quality, university professors think that the work must be excellent before moving forward. To set and adhere to strict deadlines for oneself takes a driven personality, which is not that common in the slow-moving life of academia.

Naturally, all of this waiting can become extremely frustrating. For me, it took everything I could muster to stay sane—my twin brother and my next-door neighbor suffered the brunt of the complaints. Back then, I wanted to make daily, steady progress toward completing my degree, but it seemed as if I were always waiting on someone else in order to take a simple baby step forward. However, waiting is a just part of getting a PhD. It's all a part of the academic game.

So be sure to stock up on plenty of patience and motivation before you begin your PhD program. And make the right choices before you start, so you're not waiting forever for some simple feedback.

HOW TO DEAL WITH STRESS

I think much of the stress I encountered during the pursuit my PhD was due to the way I viewed my life as a graduate student. A few years into my degree, I started to feel like I was putting my life on hold. There were so many things I wanted to accomplish, but I felt as though I was restrained from doing those things because I first had to complete my degree so I "could move on with my life." Also, I had moved to a place I didn't want to live for the sole purpose of getting the degree, and all I could think about was getting done as quickly as possible so I could start living near the beach in southern California. Recognizing my unhappiness, one of my friends who was completing her PhD in clinical psychology—as a stressed graduate student, it's always helpful to know someone in psychology—said to me, "Jason, why are you putting your life on hold? This *is* your life." Sometimes, it really is hard to see the forest through the trees, even when the forest is in your own backyard.

Now, one of my favorite things to do as a coach is give pep talks. In my opinion, the pep talk is a lost art, but it's also one of the most important duties of a coach when getting his or her athletes ready for a competition. What the coach says and how he or she says it can have a dramatic effect on the athletes. The pep talk represents the coach's last chance to motivate and inspire his or her athletes to perform in ways they never thought possible before. While working on my PhD, there were a number of times when I could have used a pep talk from my advisor; but I found that I had to be my own coach and give myself my own pep talks during the periods I was most frustrated—before my qualifying (comprehensive) exams, while waiting for my advisor's feedback on my dissertation proposal, and while writing my dissertation, for example. To stay on course and energized, try to find your own coach who can give you those pep talks during the times you get frustrated or stressed.

CHAPTER 2

Thinking Like a Doctoral Student

"Did you ever stop to think and forget to start again?"
—WINNIE THE POOH

What does it mean to think like a doctoral student, and how exactly do you know whether or not you're thinking like one? Is thinking like a doctoral student different than thinking like a normal person? What do doctoral students do that makes them unique?

Many people go through their daily lives without really thinking too deeply about countless issues. If you sit in a public place and listen to the conversations that people have with each other, you'll notice that most of those conversations are superficial in nature. People tend to talk about smaller things rather than major thoughts or monumental feelings. We get so wrapped up in our busy lives (and spend too much time watching TV) that we spend little time actually thinking.

Look at the books people read. When most people graduate from college, they usually don't continue reading the kinds of texts they were "forced" to read while in school. For example, how many people do you know who read Shakespeare in their free time? Or physics textbooks? Or essays on literary theory? Instead of reading the works of great scientists, philosophers, sociologists, economists, among numerous other legends, people read romance novels, Dr. Phil's latest weight loss book, or *People* magazine to find out what Britney Spears has been up to recently. With all due respect to romance novels, Dr. Phil, and Britney Spears, reading these things doesn't do much for your brain or your own personal development and enrichment. Except for pure, cheap entertainment value, they're largely a waste of time.

As a doctoral student, however, you'll spend a lot of time reading and thinking about what you read. During the time you spend on your degree, you're expected to eventually become one of those scholars whose work you've been reading the last four or more years.

When I was in high school, I attended a track and field camp where a former Olympian and coach would say, "Those who know why will beat those who know how." For some reason, this statement stayed with me for a long time, but it wasn't until I began graduate school and taught undergraduate classes that I realized this statement also applied to graduate students. In fact, there is a striking difference between how undergraduate and graduate students think. While undergraduate students want to know what and sometimes how, graduate students want to know why. Basically, as an undergraduate, you learn what is already known, but as a graduate student, especially as a doctoral student, you learn to add to the body of existing knowledge in your discipline. You know you're thinking like a doctoral student if you like studying a subject so specific that you can discuss it with only five other people in the world. Below are some examples of the difference between how undergraduate and doctoral students think:

Undergraduate Student	Doctoral Student
Is that going to be on the test?	If I start studying now, I should be prepared for the test in four weeks.
How many pages does the paper have to be?	The paper should be as long as it needs to be in order to say what you need to say. Generally, the longer, the better.
Do we have any homework?	What reading should I do to prepare for the next class?
How am I ever going to write a four-page paper on the Civil War?	I can't wait to get started on my 200-page dissertation on the structure of DNA in African elephants!
I can't wait to go out and get drunk this weekend!	I can't wait to spend my weekend in the library working on my dissertation concerning the structure of DNA in African elephants!
I can't wait to graduate and get a job and make lots of money.	I could stay in school forever.
I wonder if she likes me.	I wonder if she likes atomic physics.
I really don't want to go to my statistics class today.	I think I'll sit in on an extra statistics class this semester so I can learn more.

You'll find that your first few years of graduate school are spent becoming knowledgeable. By the time you finish your PhD, you may be just beginning to think independently and come up with ideas of your own.

Or you may not. There are no guarantees that when you finish a PhD program that you'll be an expert, independent thinker. That responsibility is yours. Unfortunately, most professors spend too much time in their classes teaching facts and concepts and not enough time teaching students how to develop thinking skills. Liberal arts majors have it a little better in this regard; at least they spend more time working on their analytical skills. In my opinion, all doctoral programs should include at least one required critical thinking course in their curriculums.

Obviously, you have to be intelligent to think like a doctoral student. But intelligence alone is not enough. You have to be able to build on your understanding of concepts and discover the "why." You have to be able to create logical arguments; you have to be able to think independently; and you have to persevere. Just take a look at some of the steps involved in thinking like a doctoral student.

I THINK, THEREFORE I AM...A DOCTORAL STUDENT

Impressed with my master's degree advisor's ability to come up with ideas of his own about how and why skeletal muscles work the way they do, I once asked him where that ability came from. Thinking he would spout off something like, "That's why

I'm the advisor and you're the student," I was surprised when he said, matter-of-factly, "Years of research."

If there was one thing that haunted me throughout the latter stages of my doctoral work, it was the expectation of me to "think like a scientist," a mentality with which I struggled for a long time. While people I knew in nonscientific disciplines or outside of academia perceived me as a scientist, it seemed to me that my doctoral committee wanted something more. That was when I began questioning what it meant to "think like a scientist."

Thinking like a doctoral student is not specific only to scientific disciplines. When I asked one of my friends who was getting his PhD in the department of communication and culture how he was expected to think, he replied, "like a rhetorician," which may be even harder than thinking like a scientist!

THINK BIG

The first step in thinking like a doctoral student is to think big. No one has ever achieved something great without first believing it could be achieved, however seemingly impossible at first. A couple of years after finishing my master's degree, I attended a conference for the International Society of Biomechanics. The keynote speaker at the conference was Andrew Huxley, the Nobel Prize–winning discoverer of how muscles contract and a legend in the field of muscle physiology. Naturally, I was excited to hear him speak, as I had read much of his work while working on my master's degree. One day at the conference, there was a student-only luncheon with Dr. Huxley. We all piled into a conference room at the convention center like we were waiting to talk to Santa Claus at the shopping mall. As we ate lunch, students from all over the world asked Dr. Huxley, now a man in his eighties, specific questions about muscles, the research he had done, and what he felt still needed to be learned about the way muscles contract. The intensity was palpable. Being the smart aleck that I am, but also genuinely interested in his word, I raised my hand and asked, "What was it like to win the Nobel Prize?" Amid the chuckles from the audience, this elderly man with white bushy eyebrows said in his English accent, without hesitation, "It was great. I recommend it to anyone."

While you may never win a Nobel Prize like Andrew Huxley, or a Pulitzer, or any other kind of award bestowed for great scholarship, if you're going to think at all, you might as well think big. A PhD is the highest academic degree conferred by a university, after all. Believe it or not, despite the greater salary, prestige, and respect given to MDs, a PhD is considered a higher academic degree by most. Less than 1 percent of the population has PhDs, so if you have one, be proud; it's a big deal.

As a doctoral student, professors will undoubtedly challenge you to think about subject matters at a higher level than you did while working on your bachelor's or master's degrees. Thinking big starts when you choose a school. As mentioned in Chapter 1, if you want to be the best, you should rub elbows with the best. If that means moving across the country or even moving to a completely different country to pursue your PhD, then do it. The experience and knowledge you'll gain will definitely be worth the trip.

Keep an open mind when taking classes and doing research. Study the ideas of the "big players" in your discipline. If you study enough big minds, you might just start getting a big mind yourself. When it comes time to decide on a topic for your dissertation, don't be afraid to come up with some big (but manageable) ideas. A big idea can always be pared down to a more manageable one, but a small idea cannot be molded into a bigger one so easily.

ASK WHY

The second step in thinking like a doctoral student is to ask "why?" There are many people in the world who are very knowledgeable about specific topics. Your next door neighbor, for instance, may know lots of trivia about model trains or the Civil War or gardening. The pristine garden next door that makes the neighbors envious as they struggle with their straggly weeds would make you think that your neighbor has an award-winning green thumb. At the same time, that knowledge of gardening could come from any one of a half dozen coffee table magazines on the subject, like *Garden Compass*, *Garden Style*, or *Backyard Living*, but does your neighbor know why she uses clay soil instead of sandy soil? Does she know why certain plants that flourish in the shade outdoors need light if they are placed indoors? Just because your neighbor's garden looks great doesn't mean that he or she knows why it looks great and continues to grow.

There's more to learning how to think than acquiring information about a subject. Magazines, or even most textbooks for that matter, do not teach you *how* to think. Lasting knowledge comes from understanding; so always seek to understand your subject of choice. If you have questions about something, ask your advisor, professors, or fellow graduate students. Really try to understand concepts, theories, and arguments rather than just memorize them.

UNDERSTANDING WHY

In his book, *Why We Run*, zoologist and long-distance runner Bernd Heinrich, PhD, writes, "In the same way that a painter must know the technical effects of color combinations, techniques of paint application, shading, and highlights, a runner must acknowledge physiology, the medium through which excellence is exerted." As a coach, I've always believed that understanding the "medium through which excellence is exerted" makes me a better coach. By understanding why, I have grown to think outside the box, and I've been able to integrate my own ideas into training athletes rather than by simply copying the training of other successful athletes, conforming to traditional practices, or arbitrarily engaging in trial and error, things that many of my coaching colleagues do regularly.

Whatever career path you choose to pursue after completing your PhD, understanding the many "whys" of your discipline will enable you to succeed and educate others, too.

UNDERSTAND THE LITERATURE

The third step in thinking like a doctoral student is to understand the prior body of work in your specific area of study. Before you can develop your own ideas, you first need to understand what research has been done before you entered the field—believe it or not, people were doing research long before you were born—and that requires a lot of reading. That said, if you don't wear eyeglasses before starting your PhD program, you may have to wear them by the time you finish. What are the major thoughts and arguments for popular topics in your discipline? Have these thoughts and arguments changed over the years? If so, why have they changed? What new information exists that didn't exist before? Gaining knowledge of your discipline and establishing yourself as an authority are necessary to successfully move forward.

My doctoral advisor would always ask me, "Jason, how do you know what you know?" This is a good question, and it's something you should ask yourself regularly as you pursue your degree. Do you know what you know because an authority figure told you? Because you read it? Because you researched it yourself? Because your wise grandmother told you one day? How can you trust what you know? Is it dogma? My advisor seemed to think I carried a great deal of dogma around with me. Admittedly, it's hard to "wipe the slate clean" once you've learned something and you adamantly believe you understand the subject a certain way; but it's important to keep an open mind, especially because that's the only way you can truly learn.

BE CRITICAL

The fourth step in thinking like a doctoral student is to be critical. Don't believe everything you read and don't take everything at face value. How does your neighbor know that everything he or she reads in those gardening magazines is right? My education in exercise physiology affords me some critical insight when I read fitness magazines. Often, I read things that are inaccurate or blatantly wrong that the general public would never notice, one of my favorites being that muscle weighs more than fat. Although consumer magazines have a responsibility to provide accurate information to their readers, that responsibility is sometimes overlooked in the name of simplicity, time, and ignorance.

A common mistake made by the popular media is to take the results of a single study and present them as if those results represent the whole truth, announcing them to the general public as established fact. Sometimes, the media will also misinterpret a study's findings and misinform the public, telling them the study found something that it did not in fact evidence. This is done all the time. I've even seen my own research misinterpreted by editors of fitness magazines. Imagine how frustrating it is to a researcher to open a national magazine and read something about his or her study that isn't true! How many times have you heard on the evening news about the latest food that prevents cancer? (Just for the record, no single food prevents cancer. Cancer doesn't work like that.) Typically, the producers of the evening news will get hold of a press release of a recent published study and run with it that night. That's an obvious example of how not to think like a doctoral student. As a doctoral student, you need to read all of the studies that have examined that specific food's effect on the development of cancer, what it is about the food or about how the ingredients in the food function in our bodies that causes the effect, and find out if all the studies agree or disagree. Then, you need to be critical and ask questions, such as:

- What were the populations of these studies?
- Were the samples from each study representative of the population?
- Are the results from each study only applicable to a specific population, such as patients with stage 1 or stage 2 cancer or patients with only a specific type of cancer?
- What percentage of subjects was actually affected by the food? Ten percent? Ninety percent? How much variability was there in the subjects' responses to the food?

- Was it the food itself that was the reason for the cancer remission, or was it something else?
- Did the studies have enough statistical power to detect an effect?
- Who funded the study? Was it the company that produces the food used?

None of these questions will be answered on the six o'clock news, but the answers are still important, especially since you'll only understand the whole picture after you've critically reviewed all of the studies. While the evening news may report that "a study out of France found that chocolate prevents cancer," that may only be the case if you eat a thousand grams of dark chocolate per day—chocolate, unfortunately, does not prevent cancer as we know.

Of course, being critical of fitness magazines or the evening news is one thing; being critical of scholarly work is quite another. As a doctoral student, you must also be critical of the published academic journal articles in your discipline. Just because an article is published doesn't mean it doesn't have flaws. If you're in a liberal arts discipline, be critical of the author's arguments. Is the argument logical? Does it draw upon past research? Does it use facts to support the arguments presented? Does it hold up to the scrutiny of other academics? If you're in a scientific discipline, be critical of how the described experiment was performed and the conclusions drawn from the results. Here's a list of questions you should ask yourself when reading scientific research articles:

- Is there a well-defined research question that can be answered using the study design?
- Was the type of research design employed appropriate?
- Could a better research design have been used?

- Was there enough power to detect an effect of the experimental treatment?
- Was there an adequate number of subjects participating in the study?
- Were the methods employed valid (i.e., do the methods measure what they are purported to measure) and reliable (i.e., if the study's methods were repeated, would you get the same results)?
- Was there a control group?
- Was the study cross-sectional or longitudinal?
- Were the subjects randomized to the intervention and control groups by a method that ensured the assignment was random?
- Were the characteristics of the subjects in the groups similar at the start of the study?
- Were the subjects and/or researchers kept blinded to which treatments/interventions were used?
- Were all subjects accounted for at the end of the study? If not, how many subjects were lost and for what reasons? What impact could lost data have had on the results?
- Was the study intervention the only difference between groups?
- Were the methods described with sufficient detail to be repeatable by others?
- Were there any confounding variables that could have affected the study's results?
- What procedural and/or statistical methods did the researchers use to control confounding variables?
- Other than the treatments/interventions used, what other subject characteristics could have affected the study's results (e.g., age, sex, race, etc.)?

- Do the researchers report all relevant results or just the significant ones?
- Is it possible that the results occurred by chance?
- Are the authors' conclusions logical and reasonable based on the study's results, or are they mere speculation?

When you first begin your doctoral work, you may not be able to ask these questions because you may not know better. For instance, you may not know that a repeated measures research design, in which each subject experiences all of the experimental conditions and serves as his or her own control, is more powerful, and therefore better than, an independent groups research design, in which subjects are divided into groups, with each group receiving a different treatment. Note that you must have a separate control group that doesn't experience any of the experimental conditions for the latter design. But even this knowledge is not enough. You need to understand why the first research design is better. That's why you spend your first few years learning, absorbing information, and contextualizing that information before engaging in your own independent research. This is not an easy or fast process, which is one of the reasons earning a PhD requires so much time.

REASON

The fifth step in thinking like a doctoral student is to reason your way through a problem. People are confronted by problems every day—everything from coming up with an advertising campaign at work to a leaking roof at home. How you think your way through those problems is what matters and will largely determine your level of success. Say you're presented with a problem or question in your discipline. First, write down what the problem or question is as concisely as possible. Second, write down what you know based on your general knowledge and the literature you've read. Next, write down what you don't know. Then, go find out what you don't know. Analyze those new facts. Finally, use logic to guide you toward an answer to the problem. Here's an example from my doctoral qualifying exam:

Problem:

What are the limiting steps to oxygen transfer from the air to muscles? Which of these steps is most limiting?

What I Know:

1. Sites of oxygen transfer:
   - Air to lungs
   - Lungs to pulmonary capillaries
   - Pulmonary capillaries to arteries
   - Arteries to arterioles
   - Arterioles to muscle capillaries
   - Muscle capillaries to mitochondria

2. What affects oxygen transfer at these sites?
   - Barometric pressure—the higher the pressure, the greater the driving force for diffusion from the air to the lungs.
   - The surface area available for gas exchange between air and blood in the lungs.
   - The difference in the partial pressures of oxygen between the alveoli and arteries, which determines the adequacy of pulmonary oxygen transfer. The partial pressure of oxygen in the alveoli in the lungs depends on the fraction of inspired oxygen, the barometric pressure, and the partial pressure of

carbon dioxide in the alveoli. If the alveolar partial pressure of oxygen falls, so does the arterial partial pressure (which is downstream from the alveoli) and, consequently, the saturation of oxygen in the blood. Arterial partial pressure of oxygen could be reduced as a result of a decreased alveolar partial pressure of oxygen or an inequality between ventilation and perfusion (blood flow) in the lungs, which would cause less oxygen to enter the blood leaving the lungs.

- Stroke volume and heart rate, which determine how fast blood transits the lungs.
- Red blood cell volume and hemoglobin concentration, which determines the oxygen transport capacity of the blood.
- The number of capillaries that perfuse the muscle fibers, which determines the time available for diffusion as blood transits the capillary network.
- Capacity of cells to extract oxygen from the blood, which depends on how many mitochondria there are in the muscles.

What I Don't Know:
- Which of these steps is most limiting?
- What seems logical?

There is probably no single limiting factor of oxygen transfer, but rather an integration of many factors. The performance of each step affects many other subsequent steps. It's logical to think that if there were a single limiting step of oxygen transfer, it would occur at the beginning of the oxygen pathway—between the lungs and pulmonary capillaries—

since the effects of any perturbation of an initial step would have a greater impact on overall oxygen transfer than a perturbation of a latter step, an early perturbation creating a snowball effect, with each subsequent step being negatively affected in a progressive manner. This early-step limitation is also seen in metabolism, as many rate-limiting enzymes often catalyze reactions early in the metabolic pathways. By way of analogy, if you made a mathematical mistake on the last line of your checkbook, you would have a relatively simple problem in correcting the mistake; but if you made a mathematical mistake on the first line of your checkbook, you would then have a big problem in correcting your entire checkbook and dealing with any bounced checks as a result of your initial mistake.

Even with reasoning, you may still be wrong. For example, the reasoning in the above example led to the wrong conclusion, or at least to a conclusion that needed to be clarified—it turns out the most limiting step in oxygen transfer from the air to the muscles does *not* occur between the lungs and the pulmonary capillaries, at least in healthy, inactive people at sea level, because changes in lung oxygen transfer are not accompanied by changes in maximal oxygen consumption due to the shape of the oxygen dissociation curve (i.e., it takes a rather large drop in the arterial partial pressure of oxygen to cause a significant decrease in oxygen saturation of the blood). However, in highly trained endurance athletes with high cardiac outputs (or when exercising at high altitude), the arterial partial pressure of oxygen can drop significantly, making oxygen diffusion from the lungs to the pulmonary capillaries a more limiting factor.

To think like a doctoral student, you must not make assumptions. One of the biggest mistakes I made when I first started my PhD program was that I thought I knew it all. Once you have a particular concept set in your head, it's very hard to open your mind to other possibilities and learn the correct answers. In other words, you get stuck in a rut; but to keep learning and discovering, you have to break the rules that you set for yourself. If you assume something is true, that assumption may lead to other assumptions and fallacious arguments. New research is always shedding new light on old concepts. Therefore, you must always keep an open mind. Sometimes, it's helpful to pretend like you don't know anything at all.

THINKING SKILLS

One of the best things you'll get out of your doctoral education is not the massive amount of knowledge you memorize, but rather the thinking skills you develop. From a scientific perspective, this means being able to employ the scientific method: reading with a discernible, critical eye; being able to hypothesize about something based on your understanding of the concepts in your discipline and exercising your ability to assimilate past research; designing an experiment to test your hypothesis; understanding the limitations of your research; and understanding what the results of your experiment actually mean. In nonscientific disciplines, this means being able to create cogent arguments, justifying your arguments, as well as analyzing and critiquing theories. These are skills that have merit far beyond the ivy-covered walls of academia. Everyone, not just doctoral students, can benefit from being able to think like a doctoral student.

CHAPTER 3

Tricks of the Trade

*"Tricks are for the not-so-smart, not-so-conscious part of us.
To a great degree, the highest performing people I know are
those who have installed the best tricks in their lives."*
—DAVID ALLEN

My doctoral advisor used to say that if earning a PhD were easy, everyone would do it. While the pursuit of the PhD does have its difficulties and stressful moments, there are some tricks of the trade few people tell you about that can make things a bit easier.

LEARN FROM YOUR EXPERIENCES

When I was in eighth grade, I broke the school record for chin-ups. I still have the certificate of achievement from the school's principal proudly displayed on my wall, and I still brag about that accomplishment to others. It doesn't matter that it was so many years ago or that some tough kid has probably come along since to break my record. At the time, I had the strongest biceps and forearms in junior high. I used chin-ups to show off to the girls in class. My mother even bought a chin-up bar and attached it to my bedroom doorframe so I could train at home. I did chin-ups every day. What I learned from my chin-up training is that there is a trick to doing lots of chin-ups—do them quickly. The longer it takes to do each rep, the harder it is to do many of them, primarily because your muscles will be tensed longer.

If you're wondering what chin-ups have to do with a PhD, the answer is everything. Along with other challenges, chin-ups made me develop strategies to aid in my success. Look to your own experiences to find ways to become successful. Was there an obstacle in your life you had to overcome? How did you overcome it? Now, apply those same winning strategies to your PhD pursuit. When navigating through your degree, keep your eyes open for tricks of your own that you can use to become successful.

When I was a freshman in college, my dormitory roommate pledged a fraternity. The fraternity brothers would call in the middle of the night to get my roommate out of bed—and in the process, get me out of bed, too—and come to the fraternity house to clean the bathrooms with a toothbrush or perform some other demeaning task. At the time, I thought my roommate was a complete fool, following orders from someone else just to become a member of their fraternity. It wasn't until I was a couple of years into my PhD program that I realized I was doing much the same thing.

Many people with PhDs view other doctoral graduates as members of a fraternity, and the degree is what gets you in the fraternity. If you're lucky, you'll find people who sincerely want you to succeed and become a member. Some may even feel that your presence in the fraternity will make the fraternity stronger and better. Once in a while, you'll come across others who want to keep you out (or at least make it very hard for you to get initiated). They may feel you're not worthy of the membership. Whether they try to encourage your entry or try to keep you out, everyone around you will expect you to work very hard to become a member.

Much like my toothbrush-cleaning, fraternity-pledging room-mate, you'll learn very quickly that a PhD is a series of hoops. While my roommate pledged his fraternity for one semester, you'll be "pledging" your academic fraternity for at least four years. You'll have classes, qualifying (comprehensive) exams, a dissertation proposal defense, research, a dissertation defense, and all the specific steps in between that go along with each of these major movements toward your degree. Sometimes, you just have to give people what they want in the name of finishing your degree, so the trick becomes learning how to jump through those hoops without bumping your head. Bumping your head so many times that you get a seven-year headache is yet another example of how not to earn your PhD.

KNOW WHAT IS EXPECTED OF YOU

One of the things that would have helped me get through the PhD process more easily would have been a better understanding of what was expected of me. Looking back on my experience, I think most of the trouble I got myself into was directly a result of not knowing exactly what was expected of me. As an independent person, I did many things on my own, which annoyed my advisor. I didn't know when I was supposed to be independent—independence being what I thought was the point of obtaining a PhD degree—and when I was supposed to depend on my advisor. Make sure you're clear about what is expected of you, what you can complete independently, and for what you need to rely on your advisor.

Obviously, one of the things expected of you is that you pass all of your classes—a minimum of a B minus average is usually necessary to pass classes in graduate school. If you don't pass, you'll likely have to take the class over again, and that sucks. Luckily, I never had to repeat a course, although I came close a couple of times—those darn medical school classes! Failing a class and having to take it over again is certainly another way of not successfully obtaining your PhD. Most doctoral programs in the United States are class-intensive, so you'll likely take three years of classes. My doctoral program required ninety credits beyond the bachelor's degree. Twenty-four of those credits were dissertation credits, leaving sixty-six credits worth of classes. That's a lot of classes. By contrast, doctoral programs in Europe place a greater emphasis on research. In Europe, it is expected, and even required, that students have at least a couple of publications (or submitted manuscripts) before graduating with their degrees.

Although the only research you are absolutely required to complete in order to receive your doctorate is your dissertation, there is an implicit (and sometimes explicit) expectation that you will do more research. Of course, committees want to see that you can do serious research. While the many research projects going on in your department represent one of the many opportunities I referred to in Chapter 1 and getting your name on as many abstracts and publications as you can will look good on your résumé (especially if you are planning on applying for a faculty position at a university), you have to balance your interest in taking advantage of opportunities with the need to complete your degree. This is something with which I struggled; balancing many classes with research can be a real challenge.

One of my fellow grad students once told me that I should have more than just my dissertation as a publication when I graduate. "Why?" I thought. Although having as many publications as you can is arguably important when applying for faculty positions (the infamous "publish or perish" philosophy discussed in Chapter 4), getting a full-time faculty position at a big-time research university was never my goal, unlike many of my peers. Plus, I already had dozens of publications, albeit of the commercial magazine variety, for which I was getting paid quite well.

If you're clever and think like a doctoral student, you may be able to get two or even three publications just from your dissertation alone. Sometimes, it's hard to convince yourself that spending time and effort on extracurricular research is worth the time away from meeting the requirements for your degree, but extracurricular research will undoubtedly help direct your committee members' questions for your qualifying exam, which can make your exam easier (as you'll learn in Chapter 4). I would have thought that my fellow grad student, who was already over forty years old when she gave me her advice, would have been more interested in completing her degree than pursuing extracurricular research. If you're really interested in pursuing more research, you can always stick around after your degree is completed and complete more research in your field. Early on in your graduate career, find out how much research you are expected to do, and ask yourself how much time you can reasonably devote to other research while finishing your degree in a reasonable amount of time. To that end, here's a list of other questions you should ask your advisor and others:

- What types of skills are you expected to have? Computer programming? Laboratory? Interpersonal?
- Will you have an assistantship?
- If you will have an assistantship, what work will you be asked to complete? Teaching? Research? Both?
- How many hours per week will you be expected to work for your assistantship?
- How does your research fit into the overall research agenda of the department?
- Are there timelines in place for submitting your work? If so, what are those timelines/deadlines?
- How much say will you have in deciding your own dissertation topic?
- How much direction will you be given, and how much are you expected to do on your own? How independent are you supposed to be?

DIRECTING YOUR EFFORTS

Part of the overwhelming nature of the PhD degree is that there are many things to do at once, but if you learn to direct your efforts rather than get sidetracked and try to undertake too many projects at the same time, you can streamline the process and make your life as a doctoral student much easier.

Being Busy

I'm now going to say something you've heard so many times it's become cliché: we live in a fast-paced, busy society. It seems that everyone—and I mean everyone—is busy these days. It doesn't matter if the person is a surgeon or a secretary. But studies actually have found quite the opposite—that people have more, not less, leisure time than ever before—so with all of this extra leisure time, what is everyone so busy doing?

I must admit, I've never been busy, at least not in the sense that people use that word today. At times in my life, I've had a number of things to juggle, but I've never perceived myself as being particularly "busy." I've always had time to do what I wanted to do. I've been running six days a week every week since I was in sixth grade, even throughout what was supposed to be the busiest time of my life, namely working on my PhD degree. Maybe I'm just adept at planning and scheduling my day. (Or maybe I just don't work hard enough. Doctoral students, after all, are supposed to be busy.) While working on your PhD, you'll notice that, despite all the work you have to finish, there's actually a lot of wasted time. You can choose to be busy, or you can choose to be productive. The two are not necessarily the same thing.

Between attending classes and meetings, studying, completing other class work, taking part in research, and teaching your own classes, you, too, are likely to feel busy—even overwhelmed at times—so it's important to learn to direct your efforts. With all due respect to my former professors, much of the class work they assigned was "busy work." In my opinion, spending massive amounts of time on "busy work" is truly a waste of time. It's not productive. Much of what you will learn while working to earn your PhD comes from outside of the classroom anyway. As some physicist named Einstein once said, "The only thing that interferes with my learning is my education." Moreover, despite what you may have been told growing up and despite that drive that has pushed you to pursue your PhD, getting good grades is not the ultimate goal. In fact, when you apply for faculty positions, your GPA is not going to influence whether or not you get the job. Sure, you want to do well—who doesn't?—but you should ask yourself if spending twenty hours studying for your chemistry test is really worth it when you could be using that time for something else, like working on a manuscript for publication. Ask yourself how much time you really need to study for your tests. And ask yourself what you need to complete in order to advance your career. Of course, doing well in your classes is important, but it just may not be as important as getting the most out of the other opportunities. Decide what your priorities are, and then schedule them into your week.

Helping Other Students

When it's time for you to start work on your dissertation, you will need the help of your fellow graduate students because it can be difficult to run an experiment on your own. However, you need to make yourself available to help them collect data for their dissertations, too. This can be a delicate issue because you're already going to feel overworked just trying to work on your own degree. Making time to help other graduate students with their research projects may prove difficult to fit into your schedule, but remember that when you help others, you're really helping yourself. (I learned this from the Broadway musical, *Avenue Q*, which is about young professionals, shown on stage as puppets, helping each other to make it in the real world.) The time you spend helping them will pay off when it comes time for your own dissertation. In non-scientific disciplines, you won't need to conduct an experiment or collect data, which can make things a bit easier since you don't need to rely on the cooperation of others as much; but even if you won't be collecting data for your dissertation, it's still a good idea to make yourself available to other students if and when they need help because you never know what kind of help you may need in the future.

Teaching Classes

Teaching classes is another responsibility that can take up a lot of your time. Between the time spent in class with your students, meeting with students during your office hours, and grading students' tests and papers, you can easily spend over twenty hours per week devoted to your teaching responsibilities. The good news is that PhD students get paid to teach, whereas your medical school counterparts do not have teaching assistantships to help them pay for school.

However, while giving your time to your students is important and can be very rewarding, remember why you are in school in the first place: to obtain your PhD. Ask yourself if you really need to spend ten hours per week grading student papers. Since you don't get paid by the hour, you want to optimize your time by creating a schedule that allows you to address your teaching responsibilities while effectively completing the job as well. The less time you spend on your teaching-related work, the more time you have to get your own school work done.

To save time, try to teach the same classes every semester. That way, you won't have to write lesson plans for new classes all the time. Once you have an initial plan, you can simply reuse it each semester. You can also reuse the same tests rather than have to write new ones—just be careful about students cheating on tests by obtaining copies from former students. If you teach classes that are similar, use the material from one class as a template for the others.

Having to prepare everything from scratch for the classes you teach is how not to save time and one way that may hinder your efforts of obtaining your doctorate degree.

The time I spent teaching was filled with some of the most enjoyable and rewarding moments throughout my graduate degrees. I loved being in front of students, educating them, entertaining them, trying to give them something that they didn't often get from other professors—a good time while learning. I've always approached my teaching with the premise that school doesn't have to be boring or feel like a chore. The classroom experience can be fun if teachers try to make it fun rather than simply stand in front of the class and lecture *at* the students. Secretly, I often wondered if many of my professors were as boring outside the classroom when they were with their families as they were when they were inside the classroom; I used to feel sorry for their spouses, too. In short, take advantage of the teaching opportunities you have, but don't let those responsibilities minimize your devotion and the time you spend on your own degree.

Head Start on Research

In fact, a good way to get a head start on your research is to begin writing your dissertation proposal while you're still taking classes. Try to link every written assignment for your classes to your dissertation—of course, this implies that you know the topic of your dissertation before you're finished with your classes. That way, you can have much of your dissertation done by the time your coursework is finished. Although you won't defend your proposal until after you have completed all of your classes and passed your qualifying (comprehensive) exam, that doesn't mean you can't get a head start and write the proposal while still taking classes. The earlier you can discuss what exactly your dissertation topic will be with your advisor, the earlier you can direct your efforts toward completing your research. Early in your degree, you may not know the exact research question you'll end up pursuing, but if you know the topic, you can at least get a head start with the literature review of your proposal.

Managing Yourself

While all of the above may sound like a simple issue of time management, the real issue is not in managing your time, but rather in managing yourself. If you have a real sense of purpose and understand what's really important to you, you'll soon find out that you won't have problems fitting everything into your schedule. One of the reasons that students fall behind with their schoolwork is because they spend too much time attending to what they perceive as being urgent, even when it's actually not a high priority. Too much time is wasted performing tasks that don't offer results. For example, you could spend hours preparing for a meeting with your advisor to discuss your dissertation, but if the phone were to ring during the meeting, it would likely take precedence over your discussion. This happened more than once during my scheduled meetings with my advisor. Attending to what he perceived as urgent—a ringing telephone—he would answer the call and begin a conversation that would last for fifteen or twenty minutes while I sat across from him at his desk, waiting to continue our meeting.

I often wondered about the precise reasons that it took months for my advisor and committee to read my work and provide feedback. After all, a sixty-page dissertation proposal could be read in just two business weeks if your advisor reads only six pages a day. Assuming it takes an average of five minutes to read and comment on each page, that's just thirty minutes of work per day—one-sixteenth of your advisor's eight-hour work day. When broken down like this, it seems perfectly reasonable to expect your advisor to read your proposal in two weeks. If your advisor cannot devote one-sixteenth—6.25 percent—of his or her work day to one of his doctoral students, then that's a serious problem; and the root of the problem is the same as why your advisor answers the ringing telephone during your meeting. Urgent matters tend to take precedence over important ones. This is not effective, result-oriented behavior, and yet another way to neglect earning your PhD degree.

Prioritize

As you work on your PhD, each week you should write down the most important things that will help you move closer to completing your degree. Don't merely write down a list of things to do. Instead, write down your priorities. After you have articulated those things that are important, make another list of the actions you must take to accomplish each of your priorities. Recognize that there is more than a subtle difference between these two lists. Setting priorities first will help you direct your efforts because you will automatically internalize what is important to you. In addition to providing clarity, the act of writing down your priorities forces you to consider what exactly is important to you. The secondary to-do list of actions is simply a natural extension of those priorities. At first, this second to-do list might seem overwhelming, but you'd be surprised how much you can accomplish when you direct your efforts toward what is really important rather than waste time reacting and attending to unimportant things. As Robert Cooper, PhD, says in his book, *Get Out of Your Own Way* (Crown Business, 2006), "It's not how busy you are or how fast you're moving, it's how effectively you are advancing in the right direction." Remember that what really matters is not how much you undertake, but what you actually accomplish.

In the blank spaces below, write your priorities for the week:

Week of March 21–27

What's Important?

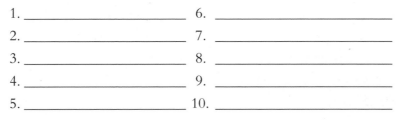

In the blank spaces below, write the actions you must take to accomplish those priorities:

Week of March 21–27

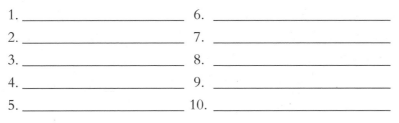

WORKING WITH YOUR ADVISOR

It's an understatement to say that the relationship you forge with your advisor is an important one. Because your advisor holds the keys to your success in his or her hands, you must get along with him or her above all else. At the same time, both of you need to understand that this is a business relationship in many ways. Personally speaking, I've even known some students and faculty who have arranged formal contracts that speak to their relationship. Most students enter into this relationship thinking that the advisor is the boss, and many advisors, like mine for example, act like they're the boss. But your relationship and your degree experience will be much more fulfilling if you both approach your degree as a mentor-apprentice relationship, in which you work together, rather than as an employer-employee relationship, in which you work for him or her. Given this arrangement, remember that you also have the power to "fire" your advisor if you feel that he or she is not holding up his or her end of the bargain.

Advisors, as you will likely be told countless times, are busy people. But since you want to learn from them and also want to complete your degree, you need to know how to work with your advisor and get the attention you deserve as a graduate student. Many times, advisors may seem like they're being dismissive or short with you when they really just have a lot on their minds. To help make things as simple for your advisor as possible and make all of your interactions count, here are some suggestions to that end:

- Learn to be resourceful (see the next section below). You don't want to ask your advisor for everything, or depend on him or her for everything. You want to be as independent as you can while still receiving guidance from your advisor.

- Give your advisor only one chapter of your dissertation or one section of your research paper at a time. While he or she is reading that chapter or section, you can work on the next one. It's much easier for advisors to proof small sections than read entire manuscripts because the perceived amount of work is less when given in small chunks.

- When you give your advisor a revised version of a paper or your dissertation, highlight the revisions you've made. If you resubmit the entire document, your advisor will have to read the entire paper over again just to find out where you made changes. If you're submitting your work via email, use the "track changes" option in Microsoft Word while you work on the paper so that all of your revisions are automatically recorded and highlighted directly on the computer screen. If you print your paper and physically hand it to your advisor, use an old-fashioned highlighter to mark the sections you revised and make notes in the margin to explain anything that needs to be explained.

- Tell your advisor the specific feedback you want. Direct his or her efforts. Ask for specific comments on each section and each chapter. If you want to know if you should include this comment or that statement, ask your advisor that specific question. If you want feedback on a specific idea that you have, ask your advisor that specific question, too. Asking questions like, "I'm having trouble with this section. Do you think my arguments are logical and relevant, or do they miss the point?" or "Am I interpreting this research or this author's arguments correctly?" can go a long way to saving you time and sparing you the feeling of being overwhelmed while working on your revisions.

- Get on your advisor's calendar before other people do. If you want to have regular meetings, schedule them in advance and get them in writing. Try to make your advisor understand how important keeping these appointments is to you.

- Keep your advisor up to date on your progress. Send him or her a quick email or slip a note under his or her door. If your advisor knows what you've been doing, he or she can better help you with your ongoing progress.

- In addition to your goals, make sure you understand your advisor's goals and expectations. Try to look at things from his or her perspective whenever possible. Understand that you are not your advisor's only responsibility.

One day, while I was discussing my dissertation with my advisor, the dean walked into the office and asked if he could "borrow" my advisor for a few minutes. I looked at my advisor in frustration, a look that was not appreciated by the dean, who later told me, "Rank has its privileges." Of course, being the smart aleck that I am, I rolled my eyes and thought, "The dean already has his doctorate. Why should he care about mine?" Looking back, I'm glad I didn't say that thought out loud, otherwise I'd probably be telling this story in the later section on burning bridges. The point of the story is that you can't get frustrated with every minor setback or delay, as your advisor does have other responsibilities and other people trying to monopolize his or her time, too.

BEING RESOURCEFUL

Part of being a successful doctoral student is being resourceful, especially when it comes to finding information or learning how to accomplish important things. For one of my biochemistry classes, my professor gave the students take-home tests with short answer and essay questions. By being resourceful, I soon discovered that many of his questions were taken verbatim from other books that I happened to have in my personal library, and a quick Internet search even revealed that one of his questions came from the website of my former advisor at a different university! Needless to say, I easily got an A in his class without having to work very hard.

Fortunately, the Internet has made the gathering of information much easier and quicker. Can you just imagine what the students of earlier generations had to endure? Much of what you'll need to find for research and classes can be easily discovered nowadays using the Internet. For example, most scientific research articles can be found using online databases like PubMed (http://www.ncbi.nlm.nih.gov/sites/entrez) and EBSCOhost Electronic Journals Service (http://search.ebscohost.com). Many journals even publish their articles online as well as in print, so you don't have to track down the journals in the library and spend time making expensive photocopies.

Others in your discipline are also good resources of information. Obviously, nobody will (nor should they) do the work for you, but many researchers (even those at other universities) are happy to answer questions that you may have. Many professors like to share their knowledge; some just like to hear themselves talk.

Email makes this exchange quick and easy. Don't be timid about emailing people with a question. I often did this while working on my degree—there was one professor at another university who was the leading researcher in the world on the topic that I was researching for my dissertation. When you email someone, first introduce yourself, and then ask the person if he or she would be kind enough to answer a few questions for you. Remember to stroke their Egos by telling them how much you value their opinions. You're more likely to get your answer that way. But be sure to do your homework first by reading his or her work; otherwise that busy professor will just refer you to one of his or her articles or books. Below are a couple of great examples of effective email queries to researchers.

Dear Dr. Nobel:

I'm working on my PhD at the University of X and have been reviewing the literature in preparation for my research project on post-exercise nutritional strategies for optimal recovery from exhausting exercise. Since you are the leading researcher in this discipline, I was hoping you could help me with a question I have. I've noticed that all of the studies examining the effects of recovery beverages on glycogen resynthesis have been done using cycling as the mode of exercise, likely due to the possible greater coupling of fatigue to glycogen depletion with cycling since the exercise is localized to the quadriceps. For my dissertation, I'm interested in using runners; however, I'm having some trouble finding glycogen-depleting protocols for runners. I have found a few: (1) 45-minute bouts of running at 65 to 70 percent of maximal oxygen consumption with 30-minute rest periods until exhaustion, (2) 70 percent of maximal oxygen consumption until exhaustion, and (3) 21 miles on a treadmill at 70 percent of maximal oxygen consumption. Some other studies have found that glycogen is reduced, but not depleted, after running to exhaustion. Do you know of any validated glycogen-depleting protocols for runners? Is it unwise to use runners for this type of research?

Thank you for your kind response.

Sincerely,

Jason Karp

Dear Dr. Laureate:

I've been reading your study from 1992 on the comparison of running economy between males and females. You explain about expressing economy as milliliters of oxygen per kilogram of body weight per kilometer when using different speeds between subjects. What is a meaningful difference in economy when expressed this way? Do you happen to know what your standard deviation was when expressing it this way? If one is to assess economy in highly trained runners, is it better to express it as ml/kg/km rather than ml/kg/min? Since you only found a significant difference in economy when expressing it as ml/kg/min at absolute speeds, which way gives you the best measure of economy? I'm doing a power analysis to determine how many subjects I need to show a significant difference in economy between two groups of subjects, so I need to find out what a meaningful difference is when expressed in ml/kg/km and what I can expect as a standard deviation. As you know, few other researchers express economy this way, and when they do, they show it in a graph and don't report standard deviations. Thanks for your help.

Sincerely,

Jason Karp

If the person is kind enough to get back to you, remember to always follow up with a thank you note. You never know when you may need that person again in the future.

Since you don't want to totally rely on your advisor for everything, it's also important to learn how to accomplish tasks on your own. Remember, independence is freedom. For example, if you're getting your degree in a scientific discipline, you may have a lot of technical laboratory work to complete. For my dissertation research project, there was a large technical component that necessitated the writing of computer software programs in order to collect and process breathing and gait signals from my subjects. Not being a computer programmer, I knew I had my hands full. My dissertation advisor, who regularly wrote computer programs for his research projects, wrote the programs for my project. While I appreciated his help, I knew that relying on him meant that my research could only progress at his rate. I also felt that I should have been the one writing the programs since this research project was for my PhD degree, but I kept my mouth shut, knowing that his help was invaluable during an already frustrating time for me. Looking back, if I had had a computer programming background, or if I had spent a few months learning how to write my own programs using the lab's software, it may have saved me more time in the long run. Bear in mind, too, that even students in nonscientific disciplines can benefit from being as independent as possible.

Another way to be resourceful is how you obtain your textbooks. The last couple of years in my PhD coursework, I didn't buy any textbooks. Textbooks are overpriced—way overpriced, especially when you buy them from your university bookstore. In order to make a profit, university bookstores mark up their textbooks by as much as 20 percent from what they paid the publisher for copies. Chances are you'll never open the textbook again after the class is over anyway. If you plan on keeping a book after the class is over in order to add it to your personal library, buy the book on the Internet instead.

Students can usually find good deals on new or used books on the Internet. You can also save money if you buy older editions of textbooks. You won't lose much content since subsequent editions of textbooks are more similar to their predecessors than they are different. You can also use the same book for multiple classes, especially when professors only loosely follow the book for their classes, which is often the case in graduate school. In all four of my graduate-level statistics classes, I was able to pass using only one basic textbook—statistics is statistics, after all, so you don't need a different book for each class. How many ways can a t-test or a correlation be described anyway? So too, with all of the information available on the Internet, you can even use the Internet as your "online textbook." When looking up facts or explanations of concepts, just be sure to check multiple websites so you know that you are getting accurate and reliable information. If you're not interested in keeping the textbook after the class is over, you can always borrow a copy from the library for free. Graduate students can typically take out library books for months at a time, even long enough to cover a semester-long course.

THE WRITING TRICK

Understandably, you'll be writing a great deal during your PhD career, so it pays to learn some writing tricks. One of the things I've learned as a freelance writer is how to get the most mileage from my articles. Many times, I simply tweak or repurpose an article, creating a new, original one that I can send to an editor at a different magazine. I've even created magazine articles (for which I was paid) from papers I wrote in school. Of course, I kept this fact quiet from my advisor since professors don't like mixing business with academia. However, there's nothing wrong with getting paid for your work. After all, you have to pay off those student loans somehow!

You can recycle papers in school, too. For new assignments, simply tweak or repurpose papers that you've already written, or you can reuse your work from other classes or even work you completed at other schools altogether. To save time and energy, try to write as little from scratch as possible. Don't worry about plagiarism—you can't plagiarize yourself. (In the publishing world, it may be "technically" possible to plagiarize yourself and get sued, but only if you relinquish your copyright to the publisher and then try to republish that same work with another publisher.) The less time you spend on class assignments, the more time you will have to pursue the many opportunities referred to in Chapter 1. Writing every paper or beginning every assignment from scratch is another way to hinder your progress earning your PhD degree.

VISIBILITY

When I was working on my PhD, there was a room down the hall from our laboratory where all of the graduate students shared desks and computers. The graduate student office, affectionately called "the dungeon" partly because it had no windows, was where the students did most of their grunt work. Personally, I think it had no windows for much the same reason as casinos don't—to keep you unaware of the time so you stay longer—unlike casinos, however, no one served us drinks. Being the recluse that I am, I often chose to finish my work at my quiet home office—or sometimes, when I wanted to be around cute coeds, the Student Union or Starbucks.

Although great work often happens behind closed doors or in dark garages (or Starbucks, for that matter), it doesn't help make you visible to others, especially your academic advisor. It's not enough to do great work; people need to see that you are actively doing great work. Successful people know how to make themselves visible. If your advisor never sees you, he or she will be less likely to attend to your needs. Your dissertation proposal will end up at the bottom of the pile on his or her cluttered desk.

In short, keep yourself busy in the lab or around the graduate student office. Volunteer to share your research at a department gathering or lab meeting. Pop your head into your advisor's office every day. Show him on what you've been working and ask to discuss it with him. The more your advisor sees your face, the more he or she will be reminded (without you repeatedly having to verbally do so) about reading your dissertation.

Unfortunately, my advisor never saw how many hours I spent working. He probably thought I was out partying, which was only partly true, but I also wanted to get my mind off of the frustration I was feeling, some of which was also lessened by redirecting my frustrated energy into the writing of this book. But having an advisor who makes assumptions about what you're doing because he does not actually see you working will definitely make your PhD experience that much more frustrating. Be visible to your advisor and your fellow graduate students, or at the very least, create the illusion of your visibility with smoke and mirrors.

Visibility is important for success in your career as well. If you want to be successful, it's important to be visible to others in your discipline. When you attend academic conferences, introduce yourself to the "big shots" also attending. Start a conversation, and ask them about their research. Academics love to talk about their research, after all. Tell them about your research; give them your business card; and stay in touch with them after the conference is over. If you're presenting your research at a conference, email the people in your discipline who you know will be attending and invite them to come to your presentation. Everyone feels good when they're personally invited to functions, even if they already planned to attend.

I once invited the editor of *Runner's World* magazine (who also happened to be a former Boston Marathon winner) to come to my presentation on the training characteristics of the U.S. Olympic Marathon Trials qualifiers at the American College of Sports Medicine conference. I knew this topic was right up his alley and something in which he would be very interested. Long story short, he came and was seriously impressed. That easily, I had made a new connection, and the editor ended up including my research in *Runner's World*.

Burning Bridges

If I had a dollar for every bridge I've burned in my life, I'd be able to pay off my student loan debt in about a week. I have a tendency to get myself into trouble. Not major trouble—nothing that broke the law—just the kind of trouble that comes from not following directions (or not being aware of what those directions are). Honestly, I like to do things, as the Frank Sinatra song goes, "my way." Many times, I didn't even realize that I was doing (or not doing) something that would eventually get me into trouble. My words and actions often rubbed people the wrong way. Admittedly, my communication style can sometimes be frank to the point of occasional rudeness. Referring to the straightforward way I went about doing things, my advisor once told me that I was like "a bull in a china shop," but at least I was unique, right?

If you disagree with the directions of others, or you're just too lazy to follow them, at least give the appearance that you are following them. Illusion can have a powerful effect—just ask David Copperfield. You'll eventually need some of the people with whom you work to become your references, especially when you apply for jobs; and family members don't count as professional references. Sadly, my reference list was down to about two people at one point.

Review the below list of things to avoid so that you don't burn too many bridges as I and some of the other graduate students I knew during my PhD pursuit had done:

- Don't send a manuscript to a journal without your advisor's approval.
- Don't alienate yourself from the other graduate students.
- Don't show disrespect or impertinence toward your advisor, even if you believe that he or she is wrong.
- Don't talk to external companies or granting agencies about getting grant money for your research without referring the person to your advisor.
- If you are using human subjects for your research, don't begin your research project without first getting clearance from your university's Human Subjects Committee.
- Don't attempt to use your research for monetary gain (at least while you're still a student).

- Even if your advisor is taking a long time to read your work, don't offer to pay your advisor to read your work.
- Follow directions, no matter how silly they may sound.
- Don't do drugs. (Always good advice.)

Many of these lessons I learned the hard way. For example, shortly after I presented some of my research at a national conference, a representative of a well-known company sent me an email expressing the company's interest in funding a future project (my dissertation). Consequently, I arranged a conference call with the representative, myself, my advisor, and another faculty member who was a part of the first study. The conference call went well, but at one point, the representative expressed the company's interest in having us add another part to our planned study, a part that addressed their interest from a marketing standpoint. She said that once we planned out the protocol of this new part and updated our budget, we should submit a formal proposal to her, which she would take to the people who decided where the grant money went. Since this new part to the study would have probably made my dissertation overwhelming, my advisor recruited a couple of master's degree students to work on the details. While I was thrilled that I wasn't going to have to complete even more work to get my dissertation done, you never want to become too dependent on other people as you move forward in your program—that's how not to get your PhD degree.

Of course, those two other students took forever to plan out the additional part of the study. More than a month later, anxiously awaiting the start of my dissertation research and knowing that my ability to begin the research was dependent on external funding—this was an expensive study with a lot of blood metabolite and enzyme assays—I asked the students to tell me what information they had gathered because "the person from Company X had contacted me about the status of things."

After receiving what little information I could from the students, I wrote an email to the company representative to whom we had spoken earlier and provided her with the information she needed to move forward. Having found out that this person had received her PhD from the same university that I had received my bachelor's degree, I also tried to subtly appeal to her as a fellow alumna, hoping she might try a little harder to secure funding for this project. Both my advisor and the other faculty member on the project found out about my little communiqué with this company representative through one of the students, and I was then called in to a conference room where my advisor and his colleague, who had perceived my little action as going behind their backs, reprimanded me. My advisor's colleague even said I should be thrown out of the university, which may have been a little harsh on his part.

I've learned that personality has a lot to do with burning bridges—maybe because I have the personality conducive for doing so. People who don't burn bridges tend to have personalities that are quiet, passive, accommodating, and nonconfrontational. On the other hand, people who burn bridges are quite the opposite, for they tend to be stubborn, short-tempered, opinionated, and extremely confrontational. These latter qualities are not necessarily always negative, but they can lead to destructive behavior if not tempered with some humility. If you find yourself in any of the above situations, it may be helpful to ask a friend or family member what he or she would do in your situation.

COMMUNICATION

A big part of getting your PhD is understanding how to build effective relationships with people. Communication is key. I've noticed that women tend to be much better at this than men. Just look at the way women talk to one another. Generally speaking, there's much more empathy and understanding among women than there is among men. Women are typically better at reading other people, listening to their side of the story, and putting themselves in other people's shoes. While cliché, men could learn a lot from women.

There will be times during your degree that you will be frustrated with your advisor and/or your committee members. How you communicate with them will make a big difference in how they perceive you. And perception is important, because their perception of you will influence their actions. If they perceive you as impatient and stubborn, they will be less likely to help you, and your dissertation proposal could fall to the bottom of their desk piles. Conversely, if they perceive you as patient and understanding, they will be more likely to help you.

When my advisor took a long time to read my dissertation proposal, I reacted to the situation by nagging him about it every chance I got. I became so frustrated with the passage of time and started to feel so desperate that I even offered to pay him to read mine. But as I later found out (from the dean, no less), all that did was offend him. Obviously, that wasn't an effective way to communicate with him. What I should have done was try to understand why he was taking what I perceived to be an unreasonable amount of time. For example, I should have said, "I really want to understand your perspective on this. Can you explain to me what the obstacles are that prevent you from reading the proposal? Is there anything I can do to facilitate the process?" While this may sound like brown nosing or lip service, it's not if you say it with sincerity and genuinely mean what you say—it's all in the intent.

Saying these things may not have any immediate effect—they may not cause your advisor to read your proposal any faster—but saying these things will definitely change his or her perception of you. Instead of thinking that you just want him or her to read your proposal for selfish reasons (because you want to get done with your degree), your advisor will think that you care about him or her and that you're willing to take the time to understand his or her busy schedule. Think about the effect that can have on someone. Instead of making it about you—even though you really want it to be about you—you can easily make it about the other person. That's effective communication, and this kind of communication takes practice.

It's far too easy to simply ask someone to do something because you want it to get done. Humans can be quite selfish by nature; but ironically, appearing unselfish to others can help you get what you want even quicker. Too bad I learned this a little too late.

MANAGING FINANCES

Let's face it: education is expensive and getting more so every year. However, it's not just the cost of tuition that makes the pursuit of a PhD so financially difficult; it's also the cost of living while you're in school for that long of a time. While the rest of society has full-time jobs to pay for things like rent, telephone bills, and electricity, being a full-time doctoral student is already a full-time job, but one without the full-time salary. The good news is that there are ways to pay for school that don't leave you with a huge debt, some of which include:

Assistantships

By far the most common way to cover the cost of your doctoral education is an assistantship, which is basically a part-time job.

Along with a monthly paycheck, assistantships usually come with a tuition waiver for a predetermined number of credits per semester. Depending on your specific discipline, assistantships are most often teaching positions, but they may also consist of research in a lab or sometimes a combination of teaching and research. In scientific disciplines, it is common for graduate students to teach laboratory classes and lower-level undergraduate classes. In nonscientific or liberal arts disciplines, graduate students typically teach lower-level undergraduate classes or help professors with grading students' papers and exams. Check with your department about your specific responsibilities that are required of your assistantship. Most departments only have a few assistantships to award each academic year, so make sure you apply for one at the same time that you apply to graduate school. Be careful, too, because assistantships usually require a separate application.

Scholarships

Most universities offer many different types of scholarships of varying amounts of money for doctoral students. Some scholarships are based solely on academic merit, while others are based on financial need. Scholarships are also awarded at different levels of the university (e.g., department, school, or university). Some prestigious scholarships, like Rhodes or Fulbright scholarships, are awarded at the national and even international level. Check with your specific department or the school of your department for a list of scholarships, their application procedures, and their deadlines. For information on Rhodes or Fulbright scholarships, visit their websites: http://www.rhodesscholar.org or http://www.us.fulbrightonline.org/home.html.

Fellowships

Harder to come by than scholarships, fellowships are typically awarded to students in high academic standing. Students are generally asked to fulfill specific contractual requirements to receive a fellowship, which may be renewable on a year-by-year basis. Fellowships are usually awarded at the university level rather than the department level.

Grants

Most universities offer grants to students to cover the expenses of their research. While this money doesn't typically go directly to the student, if the grant is awarded for your dissertation research, sometimes the money can be put toward the cost of the tuition credits for your dissertation. Special travel grants are also available to cover the cost of travel expenses of students who attend conferences and give presentations. Check with your department and school for a list of available grants and application procedures. Granting agencies or organizations external to your university are also good sources for grant funding. When applying for an external grant, take the time to put together a good proposal. The proposal is your only chance to present your ideas and to try to convince the granting organization or company that your research is worth the organization's support. Make sure your proposal clearly establishes a link between your project and the interest of the granting organization. Most likely, you will also need a letter of support from your advisor when applying for an external grant. I almost missed an opportunity to be considered for a grant that would significantly support my research because my advisor did not supply a letter of support when initially asked by the granting organization as well as myself, a problem that was only resolved when the granting organization happened to contact me directly two months later to notify me that my application remained incomplete.

Establish Residency in the State before Enrolling in School

Since public universities in the United States charge students from outside the borders of their state much more than what they charge students from within their state's borders, you'll need to decide if it's worth the time and money to spend an extra year living and working in another state while you wait to establish residency. In lieu of this plan, you may be able to fool universities by providing them with an address of a distant relative or friend, claiming that you live there. If they ask for more proof than your word, start thinking like a doctoral student. For example, having a friend in the state who is willing to vouch that you work for him or her is a nearly foolproof plan.

TUITION

For many public universities in the United States, out-of-state tuition can cost three times as much as in-state tuition. But if fifty students are all sitting in the same classroom, all being taught by the same professor, does it cost the university a dime more to educate the in-state student than to educate the student who moved to that state to learn at their school? Imagine if other services and products cost more simply because you moved to the state that had that service or product. I've been told by committees that it's done this way to encourage students to get educated in their home states,

---

hoping that, upon graduation, they will strengthen the state's economy by getting jobs there.

Students who don't plan to stay in their home states once they graduate obviously aren't going to contribute to the state's economy; but I personally think this strategy only discourages students from pursuing the best opportunities in their disciplines while also discouraging diversity in our educational system. For many universities, the definition of "in-state" or "resident" is a matter of time. You simply must have lived in the state for at least twelve consecutive months before enrolling in school to be considered an in-state or resident student. Of course, this is not the case when it concerns the state's government, which also wants your money, so it will consider you a resident for tax purposes from the moment you begin living there. Interesting how the definition of resident changes depending on who or what organization stands to make the most money.

Not only do you have to pay for course credits as a student; you also have to pay for dissertation credits. The credits for my dissertation alone cost over $14,000. All that money just to be given credit for writing a large paper, and I even did my dissertation research at a different university! University officials won't like me saying this, but you'll find that universities do whatever they can in order to get as much money out of their students as possible, claiming they have lots of bills to pay as justification. Who is going to pay for the hefty electric bill, after all? In my opinion, students (along with faculty and staff) have to pay for things they shouldn't even have to think about, like parking their cars on campus, for example. Students also have to pay activity fees, computer fees, and transportation fees, regardless of whether or not they use the campus fitness center, computer labs, or buses, respectively.

Most of my money for tuition came from a teaching assistantship and student loans. Entering my last year, I received a notice from the student loan organization informing me that they were cutting me off because I had reached the maximum allowable limit. I didn't even know there was a limit! Although I used to joke to people about all the money I owed for my education ($175,000 by the time I finished my PhD), accumulating a huge amount of debt is not a good idea. Obviously, reaching the government's limit for student loans is another way of not earning your PhD degree. Luckily, at the time I was cut off, I was already done paying for my dissertation credits, so I didn't need to pay any more tuition other than a small amount to keep myself officially registered while I completed my dissertation. To pay my monthly bills, I worked as a freelance writer and coached runners through the running and fitness coaching business that I had started while in school (http://www.runcoachjason.com). Since I was able to make money and pad my résumé by working a job that matched my career aspirations, I felt like I was cheating the system, especially when I made money for publishing articles that I had written as a part of my school work. But to be honest, it sure beat waiting tables.

Obviously, getting a PhD is a great deal of work, but it doesn't have to be as overwhelming as people make it out to be. Know what is expected of you at the outset so you can plan for all of the things you have to do. Keep your eye on the prize, and direct (or try to direct) your and your advisor's efforts. Don't try to reinvent the wheel every time. Learn to be as resourceful as you can to get things done efficiently and quickly. Be visible to and communicate with your advisor. Let him or her know that you're busy, and try to get him or her to know what you need to move forward. Learn and use the tricks of the trade in this chapter. Trust me, they will save you a lot of unnecessary stress through your journey.

CHAPTER 4

Research

*"If we knew what we were doing, it would
not be called research, would it?"*
—ALBERT EINSTEIN, PhD

Publish or perish. You can't be in academia for very long without hearing that adage (or threat, depending on how you perceive it). What you'll learn quickly as a doctoral student is that research is more important than anything else, especially at the big research universities (from where you're more likely to obtain your PhD because smaller, non-major universities don't typically have enough of a research focus to support doctoral-level research).

As an unfortunate consequence, many professors view their teaching responsibilities as something that gets in the way of their research agenda. Many professors are working at universities to conduct research, and they make it quite clear through their actions that teaching is a nuisance, a necessary evil of being a faculty member. One person I know who studies sexual dysfunction complained to me about being given three classes to teach per semester in her first year on the job. Three classes! While junior faculty members are often given a heavy teaching load, three classes are certainly manageable, especially when they are in your area of expertise. I would have thought my friend would be excited to teach impressionable undergraduates about sex! Who wouldn't?

But research remains the focus of many professors, partly because faculty are simply more interested in research because that may have been the primary reason they themselves pursued PhDs in the first place, and partly because the university system of "publish or perish" puts a great deal of pressure on faculty to deliver results, giving them little choice other than to make research their top priority. Not being available to students during scheduled office hours, not having office hours but instead meeting with students "by appointment only," and taking a long time to provide feedback on students' work are all examples of professors putting their research ahead of their students. One of my professors didn't teach the first three weeks of his biochemistry class because, by his own admission, he was too busy writing a big grant proposal for the National Institutes of Health. He instead got one of his colleagues to teach the class.

Of course, not all professors are like this. There are plenty of professors who are genuinely interested in teaching and helping students. Time also has a tendency to change professors and give them perspective, as they begin to realize that the students really are more important than achieving yet another publication from their research, as was the case with my own dissertation advisor. He once shared with me that when he first started as a faculty member, he had his own research agenda and put all of his time and effort into his research, but after a few years, he realized the valuable nature of his time when he refocused more of his attention on his students.

This change of opinion led to his "open-door policy," allowing students to enter his office whenever they wanted.

Naturally, I admired my advisor for that. If you intend on becoming a faculty member at a university after you complete your PhD program, don't ever forget that you have a chance to positively influence students' lives and the directions they themselves will take after graduation, a responsibility that shouldn't be taken lightly. Admittedly, it's easy to forget this responsibility, especially since many universities place a greater premium on research pursuits and will actually hire you based on your potential to follow those pursuits. Consequently, your teaching responsibility often takes a backseat. As a doctoral student, you're not the only one who has pressure; your professors are also under pressure themselves to crank out publications.

PUBLICATIONS

There is no question among the academic professorate that the purpose of research is publication. Your professors cannot get tenure without getting published and getting published often. Even the ones who are already tenured still regard a publication as the Holy Grail; a long publication list can lead to promotions, higher salaries, and professional prestige. As a scholar, you will not be judged by your breadth or depth of knowledge, your service-related activities, or, if you're working in a scientific discipline, your dexterity in the laboratory. No, you will become known and judged by your publications; so when it comes to a publication, everyone wants a piece of the pie.

You will hopefully become involved in other research projects in addition to your dissertation. That is one of the many opportunities you'll be offered while working on your PhD degree. On some projects, you may be the lead researcher (and subsequent first author), while on others, you may be a co-researcher (and subsequent co-author). Since the first author is the one who is most often associated with the research, the one whose name is always referenced (e.g., Karp et al., 2006), and the one who is expected to present the research at conferences, it's obviously better for your professional development to be listed as the first author on as many research articles as possible. It's always a good idea to sit down with the entire research team at the beginning of the research to determine each person's role and whose names will be on the resulting manuscript when it is submitted for publication. Although this type of open communication is common in other professional settings, it is oftentimes neglected in academia, resulting in conflict, false expectations, and hurt feelings in the end.

WHAT'S IN A NAME?

For one research project on which I was the lead researcher (and subsequently the first author on the article), it was not made clear at the outset who would be involved and what each person's role would be. In retrospect, that was my fault because I was the lead researcher; but back in those days, I (wrongly) deferred to my advisor on many issues—my take-charge attitude had already gotten me into a heap of trouble. When the research project was completed, I submitted an abstract of the study to present it at a conference. Fortunately, it was accepted, and I presented it at the conference as a poster, with the names of five others who had a hand in the research. One day, as I was writing the article to submit for publication, my then-advisor and I talked about who would be listed as an author. He had told me that while he tended to be more inclusive for the abstract and conference presentation, he was usually more exclusive for the article that would be submitted for publication. It was initially decided that only three of us who were on the poster would be listed on the article; however, one by one, the students and faculty who had their names on the poster got their names on the article, including one professor in another department who literally cried in the hallway until my advisor agreed to put her name on the article. Although her only role had been in helping secure the grant we used to fund the study, she argued that it would hurt her professionally if her name was not on the article. The perceived "need" to pad your publications list, promoted by the "publish or perish" dictum, can often lead to unethical behavior. When all was said and done, six people had their names on the published article when only three deserved to have that privilege. As I've mentioned before, everyone wanted a piece of the pie.

GETTING YOUR RESEARCH OFF THE GROUND

Doing a research project is not always as simple as it sounds, especially in a scientific discipline. Before you begin collecting data, you have to design the experiment, assemble your research team, purchase any necessary equipment and supplies, arrange your experimental setup (including the use of any computer software programs), write a brief research proposal that details your experimental design and protocol, apply for grants (if applicable), fill out Human Subjects Committee (aka the Institutional Review Board) forms, submit the forms and research proposal to the committee, wait for the committee to read your proposal, revise your proposal based on the committee's comments, resubmit your proposal to the committee, wait for the committee to approve your research, pilot test a few subjects to work out any kinks or glitches in the experimental setup, and recruit subjects for data collection.

One of the major benefits of animal research is that animals are available whenever you need them. Humans are a different story. Expect your subjects to cancel on you, and cancel repeatedly! After moving across the country to complete my dissertation research, it took over six months before I finally started collecting data.

Nonscientific disciplines are much easier to navigate, since there is no experiment to design and therefore no Human Subjects Committee needed to approve your research. Essentially, all you need is a good library. However, even working within a nonscientific discipline, you still have to endure the whole process of developing your research question, tracking down all of the literature on your topic (which may mean obtaining some sources by interlibrary loan if your library doesn't have every source that you need), writing your proposal, and discussing with your advisor and committee the contents of your proposal. One thing that is different (and sometimes more challenging) about research in a nonscientific discipline is that it can be less structured than research in a scientific discipline. Sometimes, structure can be a good thing because it forces you on a specific path. If you're entering into a liberal arts discipline, however, you often have to create that path for yourself.

Since it all starts with a very specific research question, once you have that question, the path you need to follow becomes more apparent. For example, if you want to research how men and women are portrayed by the media and the effects of that portrayal on how men and women view themselves and each other, you'll need to spend a lot of time digging in your library to find information on this topic, which can take a number of mediums, including textbooks, critical essays, audio transcripts of television newscasts, and countless other sources. Admittedly, tracking down this information may quickly become a much more difficult endeavor than finding all of the scientific research studies on the effects of aerobic exercise on the risk for heart disease.

Since most, if not all, scientific research projects are not solitary endeavors, you'll likely have to wait on a number of other people before collecting data. But aside from the often-frustrating Human Subjects Committee, other people are valuable in your research. Other people bring fresh ideas and much-needed help, so don't be shy in asking for that help.

THE HUMAN SUBJECTS COMMITTEE

For my dissertation research, which took place at a university different from where I received my degree, the Human Subjects Committee required my advisor to be present for every testing session I conducted with my subjects—I had twenty-six subjects and fifty-two testing sessions—because, in their view, since I was not a student at this particular university, the university therefore needed to protect itself in the case of a legal issue arising should an adverse event occur during testing and affect one of my subjects. Fair enough, but not having my advisor present would not have introduced any extra risk to my subjects, all of whom were performing basic and standard tests commonly performed in my discipline. What the committee didn't realize (or didn't care about) was that their decision would slow my progress, as I was only able to engage my test subjects in the lab when my advisor was available.

After a few weeks of testing subjects only when my advisor was present in the lab, he realized that his undependable schedule was causing unnecessary delays in data collection and wrote a letter to the Human Subjects Committee requesting that I be allowed to test subjects without his presence at the lab. The committee didn't like this challenge to their decision and halted my study until they could review the matter. I had to cancel my subjects' appointments and waste even more time.

Needless to say, I was frustrated. This was not the first time I had experienced problems dealing with the Human Subjects Committee, and I knew it wouldn't be the last. The responsibility of the Human Subjects Committee is to assess risk to the subjects and ensure their safety and confidentiality. Too often, however, they go beyond this simple job, fabricating risks that don't exist, requiring that unnecessary changes be made to the research protocols, and making superfluous decisions that cause unnecessary delays. Ask any college professor in a scientific discipline about his or her dealings with the Human Subjects Committee, and he or she will talk your ear off. Having your dissertation stalled by the

Human Subjects Committee so it can deliberate about risks that don't exist is yet another way how you can hinder your PhD progress. One student I knew who was working on his master's degree at the same time that I was working on my PhD research ended up never completing his master's thesis because the Human Subjects Committee gave him so much trouble about his research. Having already accepted a job in another state, he left school and eventually received an MA degree instead of his intended MS degree.

INTELLECTUAL PROPERTY

While working on your PhD, you're going to generate tons of written work, some of which will be based on your own ideas. Therefore, it's a good precaution to protect your intellectual property.

There are four main categories of intellectual property: patents, trademarks, designs, and copyright. While the majority of your doctoral work will fall within the copyright category, patents, trademarks, and designs may also apply to your work if you are working in a discipline in which you will design or create things (e.g., architecture, engineering, dramatic arts, among others).

Universities, and many professors, are very possessive when it comes to intellectual property. When I was working on my PhD, my advisor seemed to think that he owned the intellectual property and the research of his students, even when the research was the student's idea. However, this is not consistent with U.S. law or university regulations concerning graduate faculty and student intellectual property, and thankfully, such regulations exist to prevent faculty from exploiting their students for their own benefit.

If a research idea is yours, the intellectual property is yours as well, as long as you write it down. Even if the research idea is your advisor's, ideas or research topics cannot be copyrighted. No one owns them, and the same is true for any other idea. For example, if you have an idea for a song that you sing in the shower, you don't necessarily own that song. If you have an idea for a new flavor of toothpaste—chocolate chip, for example—you don't own that idea, either. Only the tangible representation of an idea can be copyrighted, namely the written, recorded document, so if you have a good idea, make sure to write it down or record it.

I once overheard an undergraduate student tell her whole class about her idea for a toothbrush that contained the actual toothpaste inside the handle so that one could simply squeeze the paste into the bristles, which would effectively eliminate the need for a separate tube of toothpaste. Not a bad idea, but she potentially made a costly mistake by verbally sharing her idea with thirty or so other people. Unless she had that idea written down somewhere, anyone else in that class (or even someone like me passing by in the hallway) could have taken that idea, designed and produced the product, patented it, and taken it to the marketplace. Just as soon as you write your idea down, it's automatically copyrighted. You don't even need to register it—so don't even think about stealing my idea of chocolate chip toothpaste. For greater legal protection, however, and for the ability to prove that the idea or the work is yours, you can register your material with the Library of Congress through the United States Copyright Office (http://www.copyright.gov) for a nominal processing fee ($35.00 for online registration, $50.00 for paper registration).

If you show your work to others, include the copyright symbol with the year and your name (©2009 Jason Karp). If you write an article for publication in a scholarly journal, you will be asked to sign a transfer of copyright form for the publisher that accepts your work. As the researcher, you still own the data, and you may use the data in whatever way you choose, whether in other works or for teaching purposes. However, the publisher retains the copyright, which means you no longer own the work and are not allowed to publish the article anywhere else without the written permission of the publisher. Bear in mind that many publishers outside of academia pay writers for the rights to their works as well.

BE CAREFUL ABOUT YOUR RESEARCH

Less than two months after I had completed my degree, I received a phone call from a friend informing me that a study I had done a few years earlier was being repurposed by my old advisor and his colleagues, using an online survey that I had written for my study and already copyrighted. I was never asked by anyone for my permission to use the survey, nor was I informed that they wanted to pursue a follow-up study on the same topic. What I was more upset about, however, was that they were essentially copying my idea, using my copyrighted work to pursue what was basically the same study I had already done and published, all to further their own careers without including me or giving me any professional acknowledgment. They did this under the guise of "extending your research findings," as they said. The whole thing just smelled fishy. Instead of being up-front with me, they went behind my back and attached their names to my work. They should have contacted me and informed me of their interest in using the survey for their study, which is required by United States copyright law.

On another occasion, one of my former professors had copied paragraphs verbatim from one of my published papers and pasted them into his column for a national consumer magazine, a column for which he was paid. While he had been listed as the fourth of six authors on the paper that had been published in a scientific journal a couple of years earlier, I did all of the writing and revising as the first author, and the copyright now belonged to the journal publisher. One day, browsing a bookstore a few months after I graduated, I was flipping through the pages of a magazine and found his column only to notice that it contained my writing! Even if there are multiple authors listed on a published paper, taking someone else's writing and claiming or selling it as your own is the definition of plagiarism. This kind of thing happens more than you may think. Unfortunately, the graduate students who generate much of the research at their universities often pay the price, so if an idea is yours and you're doing all of the work for your study, take whatever steps you need to make sure you are protected. Find out what the policies are regarding research and intellectual property from your academic department, the university graduate school, or the university's legal counsel before you start any research.

AUTHORSHIP VS. CONTRIBUTORSHIP

By definition, an author is someone who writes. In academia, however, the term "author" is given a broader definition to mean "anyone who has actively taken part in the research." An author should take intellectual responsibility for the research that is being described in the written form. As such, he or she should have an intimate relationship with the research. A contributor, on the other hand, gives or adds something to the research, such as financial support, feedback on the draft of the article, among other contributions. While many advisors seem to think that being a contributor warrants their names to be listed as one of the authors, this is not always the case. Writing the article warrants the person's name to be listed as an author; contributing to the research, either by adding something or providing feedback, warrants an acknowledgment at the end of the article. It wasn't until after I changed advisors and embarked on my dissertation that I realized the difference between authorship and contributorship. You could say that I was led to believe that the advisor automatically gets his or her name on an article and more than just a mention at the end.

Oftentimes, academic advisors and professors get published by riding on the coattails of their graduate students. I have known many scientists in my discipline who have somehow gotten their names splattered all over the literature simply because they have a number of doctoral students working under them. Although not entirely ethical, this is just the way it's done. With this point of view, the student's research is also the advisor's research. Typically, the advisor will be the final author listed on an article as the person who oversees the research and as the corresponding author in dealings with the journal's editor and publisher. If there are more people involved in the research other than you and your advisor, the order of names on the article should be decided among all the co-authors before the article is written. The advisor may have had the initial idea, but as the student, you'll write the grant proposals, carry out the research, write and revise the manuscripts, and submit them for publication. Sometimes, you may have the idea yourself, which you bring to your advisor to help you develop and shape. A good resource on the ethics pertaining to authorship and the submission of scientific manuscripts is the International Committee of Medical Journal Editors (http://www.icmje.org).

If you are the lead researcher and first author on a manuscript that you intend to submit for publication, do the best you can to manage the project. You are not obligated to wait on your advisor for his or her approval or permission to submit the manuscript, despite what he or she may tell you. As a student, you pay tuition to the university, and in return, you should receive educational support, which includes the forum to conduct research. Therefore, after the manuscript is completed, politely ask your co-authors and advisor for final feedback and give them a time frame for their replies.

TIME PROBLEMS

Once, I waited ten months for my advisor to provide his final feedback on the third draft of a manuscript on which he was the second author. After I had moved across the country to complete my dissertation at another university, I brought this issue up with my new advisor and he suggested I give my former advisor one more chance to give me his "stamp of approval" to submit the manuscript to a journal before removing his name and submitting it myself. On my advisor's recommendation, that's exactly what I did. I wrote to my former advisor and told him that I was still interested in submitting the manuscript and that if I didn't hear from him within one week, I would remove his name and submit it with my name alone. The week went by with no response, so I did exactly what I said I would do and submitted the manuscript with only my name, including my advisor in the acknowledgments section. Needless to say, my former advisor wasn't too thrilled. He perceived that I was giving him an ultimatum, and he tried to get me expelled from the university for what he called "academic misconduct." If there's one thing you can do to really piss off your advisor, it's to remove his or her name from a research manuscript and submit it to a journal on your own. Waiting indefinitely for your advisor's approval to submit an article for publication, however, is another way of not obtaining your PhD degree. This time issue can be a real problem if you have an advisor who doesn't get things done quickly. Hopefully, you'll never experience this problem at all, and in fact, I've known students who have experienced both fast and slow advisors.

CONFERENCES—THE PUBLIC FORUM FOR YOUR RESEARCH

Regardless of your discipline, one of the things you'll do as a PhD student is submit your research, most often in the form of an abstract (or synopsis) to present your findings at a conference. Presenting your research at a conference is a wonderful opportunity to share your research with others in your discipline, not to mention a great chance to develop yourself professionally. When you attend conferences, make sure you bring business cards and hand them out judiciously. Many academic departments will award travel grants to students to attend conferences and present their research, so be sure to check with your department about applying for these travel grants.

Conferences are also good opportunities to meet and talk with other academics, some of whom may be renowned. Most people in academia love to talk about themselves and their research, so conferences are a great place to pick the brains of others in your discipline. You can also meet other students from other universities, inquire about jobs, and watch other nerdy academics dance at the banquet. Universities and companies will often post job openings on a bulletin board at particular conferences; some will even conduct interviews at the conference for those who previously applied for the job. I've also found that conferences are good places to get motivated, as you're among the top people in your discipline, all of whom have come together to discuss their research. Earning your PhD can be a long, arduous process, so use conferences as opportunities to light the fire in your belly and remind yourself why you're putting yourself through what may seem like torture. When the conference is over, immediately go home and start working on your dissertation.

Doing research can be very rewarding, especially since it's through research that we make new discoveries and come a bit closer to the truth. That is the single biggest thing that distinguishes the PhD from other degrees—it is first and foremost a research degree. Since you'll be spending a lot of time engaged in research, it's not enough to know about the research project itself; you must also know about all of the many legal issues surrounding it. Don't get backed into a legal corner because your advisor and his or her colleagues are pressuring you because of their "publish or perish" mentality. Many research problems can be avoided if you have a contract at the outset of each research project detailing everyone's roles.

CHAPTER 5

The Qualifying (Comprehensive) Exam

"I think, therefore I am."
—RENÉ DESCARTES

Imagine that you're standing at the head of a long, dark, oak table in the dean's conference room. A sheet of glass covers the table, the pristine equivalent of the plastic covering the furniture in your grandmother's house, placed there to protect it from messy grandchildren. You're dressed in a suit, your lucky underwear, and a tie your mother gave you for Christmas last year. Pictures of your school and of its aristocracy—former deans, presidents, chancellors—hang prominently on the walls. The heavy door is closed. The room air feels cold on your warm, clammy skin. A small ray of sunlight peeks into the room through the synapse where the velvet curtains meet, shining on the table's glass. Members of your committee sit in chairs around the table. Your advisor, the chair of your committee, begins with the first of many questions you will be asked over the next two hours: "So what's the meaning of life?"

Of course, unless you're getting a PhD in philosophy, you're not likely to get asked this question, but you may be asked questions that are just as tough; and you may be asked to philosophize, too. One student I knew who was getting her PhD in clinical exercise physiology was asked, "What is the difference between health and wellness?" She later told me she was not expecting a question like that. On the surface, this question may not seem too difficult, but what makes it difficult is that questions like this tend to catch students off-guard because they typically spend all of their time studying more concrete things like facts, concepts, or the latest research findings.

The qualifying exam, also referred to simply as "comps" because of its comprehensive nature, covering everything in your discipline of study, is a stressful rite of passage for doctoral students. The attitude of most students is "we have to know everything," which is utterly impossible. The exam itself is conducted much like a jury trial. You get asked questions; your committee members, who all seem at the moment like opposing attorneys with the stature of Perry Mason, try to rattle you. When the two hours of questioning are over, you walk outside of the room and pace the hallway while your committee deliberates, not unlike a jury. Pass or fail, not guilty or guilty— you anxiously await your verdict. I awaited this verdict three times during my PhD tenure, the stress of which nearly caused me a breakdown. Luckily, you can avoid this stress yourself by knowing as much about the process as possible before going through it. To that end, let's take a closer look at the qualifying exam, which is typically composed of two parts, namely the written part and the oral part.

THE WRITTEN EXAM

The written part of the qualifying exam can have different formats, but is typically composed of a series of essay questions from each of your committee members. No multiple choice questions, and you can forget about matching, fill in the blanks, or true/false. You're at a whole different level now.

My written exam was divided into four two-and-a-half-hour sections over the course of two days. Each section of my written exam was a set of questions from each of my committee members. Your exam could take longer or shorter—who knows? Although the exact nature of the essay questions and the duration over which you'll take your exam will obviously depend on your specific committee at your particular university, the questions tend to be more conceptual in nature rather than factual or concrete. For example, instead of being asked, "What happens to heart rate as exercise intensity increases?", your committee will more likely ask you, "How is heart rate controlled during exercise?" If there are a number of other students in your department all taking the written exam at the same time, there may be questions common to everyone in the major areas of study and separate questions for your unique minor area of study.

While it may now prevent my former committee members from reusing their questions for future students, below are some of the questions I received for my written exam in exercise physiology. These are only meant to give you an idea of the types of questions you may expect if you are pursuing a scientific discipline, as the subject matter will obviously be completely different given your specific subject of study.

- What research needs to be done to clarify the role of exercise in immune functioning?

- How can an increase in the lactate threshold be interpreted?
- Explain how hydrogen ion concentration can be given so much importance in biological chemistry despite its small concentration in plasma.
- Is cardiac performance a determinant of preload, or is preload a determinant of cardiac performance?
- What are the similarities and differences between hypoxia at altitude and hypoxia in utero?
- What are the limiting steps of oxygen transfer? Which steps limit the maximal rate of oxygen consumption (VO_2max) in people of average fitness?
- Discuss the arguments for both central and peripheral limitations to VO_2max.
- How and why does altitude affect VO_2max?
- What are the pros and cons to a strong ventilatory response to exercise?
- Estimate daily energy use for a marathon runner.
- What gastrointestinal tract processes are rate-limiting in supplying fuel during exercise?
- Describe the hormonal regulation of fluid balance during exercise.
- Explain the models of fatigue, and discuss the physiological and biochemical attributes that explain resistance to fatigue.
- How do you know if you have an experimental effect, if there really is an effect, or vice versa?

Here are some examples of exam questions for nonscientific disciplines:

- Critically evaluate both the old and the new welfare economics, commenting in particular on their ability to guide the choices of working policy economists. (Public Finance)

- The scores of Handel's Fugue in G-minor (HWV 605) and the choral fugue 'He Smote the First Born of Egypt' from his Oratorio "Israel in Egypt" (HWV 54) are provided. Considering significant aspects of fugal design and structure, discuss how Handel developed the choral movement from the keyboard piece. (Music)

- The score of the first movement of Beethoven's Piano Sonata in E-minor, Op. 90, is provided. Discuss Beethoven's use of sonata form in this minor-mode movement. How does this movement conform to the usual harmonic practice for a minor mode sonata; are there some unusual deviating features? In the exposition, where does the second subject begin, and why? Explicate the overall tonal organization of the development. What is unusual about the retransition and beginning of the reprise? (Music)

- A two-way set associative cache memory uses blocks of eight words. The cache can accommodate a total of 2,048 words from main memory. The main memory size is 128K x 32. Formulate all pertinent information required to construct the cache memory. Draw a diagram of the cache organization with all the information. What is the size of the cache memory? Explain the major difference between direct mapping cache and set-associative mapping cache. How does a data cache take advantage of spatial locality? Give an example. (Computer Science)

- Discuss the various theories of second language acquisition upon which communicative language teaching is based. What are the theoretical underpinnings of the communicative approach to language teaching? (Linguistics)

- In *The Classical Hollywood Cinema*, Bordwell, Thompson, and Staiger work from an analogy comparing the Hollywood system of film production with assembly-line manufacture. Using their work, as well as other works on classical cinema, discuss the regulated production of classical film, taking into consideration industrial, economic, and stylistic concerns. If you see limitations to the assembly line metaphor, discuss these. (Film Studies)

- Social movements such as feminism, socialism, and communism in the early twentieth century United States spawned a variety of politically engaged artistic expressions, including visual art, dance, theater, fiction, and poetry. Focusing on poetry, analyze the development of politically engaged literature at this time, making specific reference to the major aesthetic and thematic preoccupations of at least three poets. (English—American Literature after 1900)

- Aristotle believed that a speaker's voice was a tool for persuasion. Contemporary theorists in composition and feminism see voice in different and often conflicting ways. Using Aristotle or one other classical theorist to begin your discussion, analyze how the work of at least two contemporary thinkers explores the concept of voice and how their work expands and extends Aristotle's. (English—Rhetoric and Composition)

- According to Kathleen Lennon and Margaret Whitford in *Knowing the Difference: Feminist Perspective in Epistemology* (Routledge, 1994), "Feminism's most compelling epistemological insight lies in the connections it has made between knowledge and power. This, not simply in the obvious sense that access to knowledge enables empowerment; but more controversially through the recognition that legitimating of knowledge claims is intimately tied to networks of domination and exclusion." Use this observation to outline differing

critical views of language, power, and knowledge epistemology. What is gained and/or lost for the individual because
of each theory? (English—Literary Theory)

• Discuss the major political, religious, and economic indicators
of state-level societies. How can these be recognized archaeo-
logically? (Archaeology)

See why the qualifying exam is such a hard test to study for?
These questions are all over the place! Although you never get to
see how your committee grades your exam, you'll likely be graded
on how well thought-out your answers are, how you relate your
answers to the literature, and whether or not you've accurately
shown your knowledge of your discipline's current practices and
standards. Your committee members will evaluate your answers
based on your ability to intelligently discuss the most important
questions in your discipline.

The hardest part of preparing for the qualifying exam is simply
trying to predict what topics will be covered so you know what
exactly to study. Depending on the discretion of your advisor, your
written exam may also include a take-home part, for which you
will need to research some questions. For the take-home part of
my written exam, I had one week to research and write a paper that
included answers to the following questions:

• Convince your committee that you understand the inherent
principles of evolution. Do you agree that man is a successful
species? Provide references for any definitions you might use
and briefly outline the contributions made by prominent scientists throughout scientific history.

• Scientists have debated the significance of our physical traits
as far as their contributing to "man being what man is."
Among those cited as being significant are the opposable

thumb, an upright posture, an enlarged neocortex, etc. Briefly outline what you consider to be crucial evolutionary improvements and detail when these traits first show up as characteristics of modern man. Provide a bibliography that supports your contentions.

- Certainly, early man had to "compete" in order to survive. What, or rather, against whom did early man compete? And for what, in your opinion, did early man compete?

- What physiological systems are unique to man as far as "exercise" is concerned? How does man measure up against the natural athletes?

- Given the previous material you have provided as a platform, how do you explain human diversity? Can it be quantified? If so, how? As far as the ability of man to perform athletic endeavors, how does human adaptation compare to the role of human variation? Is there room for natural selection in your view of human evolution? Document your opinions by using relevant data and appropriate references.

- Do you accept the limits of performance from the notion of "symmorphosis"? Is it consistent with concepts inherent in your understanding of human, mammalian, or even eukaryotic evolution? Provide evidence for your opinion.

- With all this said, what is there to be said about the limits of human performance? How fast can someone run the mile? What determines the limit to how fast the 100-meter dash will be run? Is there a way to predict what those limits are? What running events appear to be approaching these limits, and what is the evidence of this?

To obtain my PhD degree or not, this was a lot of work to accomplish in just one week. While many of these questions were fascinating to me, even stimulating me to pursue a PhD in the first place, at the time I felt like I was simply jumping through yet another meaningless hoop. When you have this much work to complete in such a short period of time, you stop thinking about what you're doing, and you switch to automatic pilot. I was lucky I found my automatic pilot for this paper. Exactly one week, seven headaches, and thirty-six pages later, I dropped the paper on my advisor's desk and took a vacation.

Depending on your specific department's policies, it's possible that your written exam only contains a take-home part, which is not uncommon. One student I knew in the department of communication and culture had four take-home essay questions for which he had to write forty-eight pages—twelve pages for each question—in two weeks. Another student I knew who was getting her PhD in clinical science in the psychology department developed questions herself along with her committee members and had an entire summer to write answers to them! Evidently, not all PhDs are the same.

While your committee obviously cannot expect as much thoroughness for on-the-spot questions that you answer in a classroom, the thoroughness expected for take-home questions can be enormous. For example, the student I knew in communication and culture was expected to trace a detailed genealogy of the concepts of ideology and hegemony from their inception in theoretical writing to the present, and that was for just one question. He said he could read for a whole year and still not have read enough to adequately answer the question.

If your written exam has only a sit-down part that will likely last a few hours, bring some snacks to eat and water to drink with you. Wear comfortable clothes. Pace yourself through the questions—even though you'll only have about two-and-a-half to three hours for each section, which may seem like a great deal of time at first, but flies by when you're taking an exam and trying to write as much as you can.

Here's a list of things to bring with you to the written exam:

- Paper and pen/pencil. Although you may have the option of taking the written exam on a computer, it helps to have a pad of paper handy to jot down some thoughts.
- Something to eat/drink. You're going to be sitting for a few hours, and you'll inevitably get hungry. Keeping your blood glucose level from dropping will also help you to think better.
- Chocolate. You just can't go wrong with this.
- Ear plugs. If you are in a room with other people taking their written exams, you may want to block them out.

THE ORAL EXAM

The oral part of the qualifying exam, which is based (sometimes loosely) on your responses to the written part, takes place typically one to two months following the written exam—but may be scheduled either sooner or later than that as well, depending on how quickly your committee reviews your written exam answers. In turn, your committee members will each ask you questions about what you have written. They may ask you to elaborate or defend your answers, elucidate something that is not clear, or change your answer if what you have written is wrong. Note that in nonscientific disciplines, there may not be a right or wrong answer, but rather strong and weak arguments that include or lack support. Then, they'll try everything to pick your answers apart, so be prepared.

A friend earning his PhD in rhetoric in the department of communication and culture told me that his committee wanted him to stand firmly by his responses and defend them even as they told him that what he wrote was wrong. "They asked a lot of questions specifying what I meant by this term or that term, trying to get me to backtrack or contradict myself," he said. "I think they were trying to see how well thought-out my arguments were and if I'd properly thought through all the potential nuances and challenges to my arguments."

Once they have covered your written responses, your committee members may ask other questions. Typically, each round of questioning gets deeper and deeper; however, the format is not simply: question, then answer, question, then answer. It's much more like giving and taking with each committee member. For example, a committee member will begin by asking you a general question, and in response, you will try to answer. Then, he or she will build on what you said and perhaps ask you another related question. This give-and-take style will likely last for a few minutes until either that particular committee member is satisfied and has nothing more to ask this round or you've pinned yourself into a corner and can no longer provide an adequate answer.

While this may seem intimidating (maybe even downright brutal), the committee members do this not with malicious intent but rather to gauge how you think and determine exactly how far you can proceed with your line of thinking. They want you to be able to think on your feet when answering questions. They are interested in hearing how you make an argument, how you justify what you include and exclude, how you analyze and critique research, and how you employ theories to make your argument stronger. Basically, they're interested in seeing how you enter into the ongoing "scholarly conversations" about the areas in which you're most interested and how you add your own unique perspective.

It's inevitable that your committee will ask questions to which you don't know the answer, which happened to me frequently, but if you try to anticipate their questions, it can make your life a whole lot easier. One member of my committee, a professor of comparative animal physiology, in particular was rather difficult. He was a tough cookie, giving me looks during the oral exam that suggested he thought I didn't know what I was talking about—and to his credit, maybe I didn't back then. Afterward, I found out that he wasn't pleased with my performance and that he actually failed me. It was upsetting to say the least, mostly because you want to prove to your peers that you're competent at this level of academia and are worthy of obtaining your PhD degree.

But it's hard to please everyone. For the rest of my life, I'll remember that I couldn't convince that one professor that I was worthy of a PhD. But you know what? That's okay, because you can't always convince everyone. You may find yourself in a similar situation. Just remember that you usually only need a majority vote to pass the qualifying exam, so if you have a committee member who seems to be tougher to please than the others, don't waste valuable time trying to convince that one committee member that you're worthy of the degree. Instead, focus on convincing the majority.

When you get into the situation where you don't know the answer, the trick is staying calm and focusing your answer on the things you already know so that you can use that information to try to get closer to the answer for which they may be looking. It's not usually helpful to shrug and tell your committee, "I don't know," and then leave it at that. In fact, you may raise a few eyebrows that way. However, it is okay to say, "I don't know, but let me try to reason it out based on what I do know." Don't do this for the first time at your exam—this type of thinking off the top of your head takes practice with someone else in the room—so practice this way of answering questions long before the oral exam starts. Get together with other graduate students and practice answering questions from each other. Even set up a mock exam with the other students. Trying to climb this mountain on your own without the help of others is yet another example of how not to earn your PhD degree.

The oral exam can be a high-stress, pressure-filled experience, but only if you let it be that way. The problem is, like many situations in life, we often allow the pressure to get to us. So relax; just look at the exam for what it is—a chance for you to show your committee members how much you know and how well you think. The key to reducing the stress is to be prepared and know as much about the exam as you can beforehand. Think about what each committee member is likely to ask. Confidence comes from being prepared, and remember that most doctoral committees honestly want you to pass. They don't enter the room thinking, "I can't wait to fail you."

For your oral exam, make sure you eat beforehand, and don't forget to bring a bottle of water with you since your mouth will get very dry from nervousness and trying to speak. When you get asked questions, don't just blurt out an answer. Take your time and think before you speak. If it helps you to write things down, then do so. Remember, this is your exam, your chance to show your committee what you know and how you think. You're the one in control, even though it may feel like they are. Never feel rushed to answer. You dictate the pace.

Here's a list of things to bring with you to the oral exam:

- Paper and pen/pencil. You may want to jot some ideas or notes down during the oral exam before blurting out a response.
- Your lucky tie. You will be expected to dress professionally (i.e., a suit) for your oral exam. If you're a woman and don't have a business suit, wear something professional (like what you would wear to present your research at a conference). If you don't have a lucky tie or some other lucky piece of clothing, at least make sure you wear clean underwear.
- You should also bring food for your committee to the oral exam—it can definitely be helpful to find out what foods they like first. People are less irritable, kinder, and more forgiving when they've had something to eat. The way to the hearts of your committee members may not be through their stomachs, but it can't hurt. Just make sure it's the right kind of food. Bringing stale doughnuts for an exam at four o'clock in the afternoon that nobody would touch is another way how not to earn your PhD degree.

IF YOU FAIL

While many students pass their qualifying exams on the first try, some students can (and do) fail for a variety of reasons. Perhaps they weren't prepared, they got overwhelmed by the pressure of the moment, they weren't able to show the committee members what exactly it was they wanted to see, someone on the committee didn't particularly like them, or maybe someone on the committee was just having a very bad day. While the latter two reasons may seem unfair and even unethical, the fact is that people are people first. True, they may have a duty as your committee members to judge you based on the merits of your work and your ability to show them that you are a scholar; but they are also human beings, with the same human feelings and subconscious tendencies as any other person. That's why it's important that your committee members like you, maybe above all else.

The qualifying exam is not a perfect system. Sometimes students pass when they shouldn't pass, and sometimes students fail when they shouldn't fail. I've seen this firsthand.

While no one wants to fail, the good news is that failing once is not the end of the world. Don't get me wrong—failing sucks. When your committee tells you that you've failed, you feel a gigantic sting. It hurts, and it makes you feel incompetent; you even begin to question whether or not you really have what it takes to complete your PhD, but it's not the end of the world. Failing twice, however, is the end, because failing twice means you don't get to complete your PhD, at least not at that particular university.

If you fail the first time, your committee will decide whether or not you should be given a second chance. Unless they believe you have no chance of passing, you're almost always given a second chance to pass within a few months. Depending on whether you fail the written or oral parts of the exam, you may not have to take them both over again. For example, if you pass the written but fail the oral, you may be asked to take only the oral part again. If you fail the written, however, your committee may or may not require that you retake the oral until you pass the written part as well. It doesn't make much sense to take an oral exam if you haven't shown that you can pass the written exam. However, your committee may take the opposite approach and allow you to take the oral exam, hoping that you're able to cover any holes exposed in your written exam.

The qualifying exam is often used as a way of weeding out students who, their committees believe, are not at the level of a PhD-worthy scholar. Since you want to pass your qualifying exam on the first try, you want to know exactly what your committee is looking for before taking the exam. I didn't do this, and it cost me...greatly.

A QUALIFYING EXAM FROM HELL

Let me tell you a story. The first time I took my qualifying exam, I passed the written part; but during my oral exam in the dean's conference room a couple of months later, things didn't go so well. After I walked out of the room to wait for my committee to deliberate, I was still hopeful, thinking that I probably did well enough to pass. After about one hour (not a good sign), the door opened, my committee members walked out, and then they told me to go back inside, where my advisor was sitting at the long oak table with the glass top. He didn't have to say anything. The look on his face told me what was about to come out of his mouth. After my heart sank into my colon, my advisor told me that my committee decided I should take another oral exam. I felt like my back was up against the wall (and it was). I prepared the very best I could, and I walked into the room knowing that I had done everything I possibly could to prepare. How was I ever going to pass on my second try?

I took the second oral exam a few months later. This time, after waiting another hour for the committee's deliberation (again, not a good sign), the verdict came back with a tie vote—one of the disadvantages to having an even number of committee members. Of course, I was floored. I thought my degree was over. I had the inauspicious honor of being the first student in my department to have his qualifying exam end in a tie. My only saving grace was that a tie, while not constituting a pass, did not constitute a fail either. Not knowing what to do with a stalemate, my advisor went to the dean, who in turn decided that I should start from scratch and retake both the written and oral exams again. Ouch! The dean also appointed a fifth member to my committee so that there wouldn't be another tie in the future.

The doctoral students who succeed are the ones who refuse to buckle under the failures that are heaped upon them, the ones who reject the notion that they're just as mediocre as their advisors or committee members say they are. Throughout the next few months, I kept reminding myself of this. I studied as hard as I could, but more importantly, I tried to understand exactly what it was that my committee members wanted to see from me and then practiced (in front of other people no less) giving it to them. I then took the written exam again. After all of that studying, thinking I was prepared, one of my committee members asked me to summarize the research and arguments for and against the origin of life on Earth! Why a physiology professor whom I had for a class in comparative animal physiology would ask me such a question on a qualifying exam for my PhD in exercise physiology, I have no idea. I certainly wasn't doing any research on the origin of life, and he certainly did not hint to me beforehand that I should know this line of research. I think he probably spent too much time in his ivory tower. As I read that question, my level of stress went through the roof, as I knew practically nothing at the time about evolutionary biology and the origin of life.

Despite that question, I finally passed both the written and oral exams another few months later, but even this success wasn't without its sting. The professor in comparative physiology in the medical sciences department who asked the origin of life question failed me all three times. I still live with that today. Each of the three times I walked out the door to await my committee's verdict, I waited an hour, pacing the hallway, wondering what exactly was taking them so long. It was hell. From first written exam to the last oral exam, the whole process had taken me nearly a year, time that I would not be able to recoup. Having to take your qualifying exam three times is just another example of how not to earn your PhD degree.

HOW TO STUDY

Before you study for your comps, ask your committee members how much breadth and depth of knowledge they expect you to have. What kinds of thinking skills should you possess? From what sources should you study? What material do they really want you to know and understand? Since each committee member will ask you questions, I recommend speaking with each of them individually. Someone I know who did his EdD (Doctor of Education) and studied for his exams with a group told me that the group invited each professor who would submit questions to have lunch with them and then asked the professors what they should expect on the exam, what national issues in education they should understand, and what the professors had worked on previously and perhaps enjoyed some scholarly pride completing. This is a very smart idea because professors like to talk about their own research.

When I worked on my master's degree, my committee was interested in seeing how much I knew—mostly facts and explanations of theories. I had to show a mastery of the discipline, which was narrowed to the specifics of my coursework and research. For my PhD, however, my committee was more interested in how I could think critically and how I could reason my way through a problem (on the spot). They wanted to see, as I was later told, that I could think like a scientist. This latter approach was difficult for me, since most, if not all, of exams you take in school do not test your ability to think but rather to memorize, recall, and regurgitate. My qualifying exam represented one of the first times throughout my twenty-two years of schooling that I would be tested on my thinking ability rather than on my ability to memorize, recall, and regurgitate.

To study for the written part of your qualifying exam, read and think as much as you can. You may want to begin your studying by reading select chapters from a textbook to review the basic concepts in your discipline. Just like millionaire athletes who always practice the fundamentals of their games, so too should you return to the basic concepts in your discipline. It's from these basic concepts that you can build a solid foundation and give thorough answers.

Make a list of important issues in your discipline, and understand the different takes on the issues from prominent researchers. In any scientific discipline, there will be contradictory findings in the literature, mostly because people employ different methods for their studies. Understand why the findings are contradictory and what the salient conclusions are. Reading review articles helps immensely, especially since these articles, which are typically written by a leading researcher in the area, do an excellent job of critically reviewing and summarizing the literature.

Even with all of this reading, accept the fact that no matter how much you read, you will inevitably be asked questions on material you didn't study—there's no way of knowing exactly what to study for these questions, after all. That's what makes the qualifying exam much harder than any other exam you'll take, and that's why you need outside help to predict as much of its content as you can.

Ask other students who took the exam before you what questions they were asked. Although you likely won't be asked the same questions, you will probably receive the same types of questions, especially if you have the same committee members. If you've been involved in research by the time you take your qualifying exam, expect your committee members—most likely your advisor, since he or she will be the one most familiar with your work—to ask questions based on your research. They may not ask particular questions about your research projects, but they may ask questions about the topics. For example, if you are doing research on estrogen replacement therapy and breast cancer, you may be asked a question about how estrogen plays a role in the development of breast cancer, whether research supports or refutes the use of estrogen replacement therapy for postmenopausal women, and what more research needs to be done in this area. These would be good questions because they require an understanding and application of the underlying physiology, some knowledge of the research in this area, and your ability to think like a scientist.

Therefore, it's a good idea to be involved in research so that at least one or two of the questions on your qualifying exam are somewhat directed to the areas you know (assuming you know about the research you're pursuing). If you are not doing any research, you leave the door open for your committee members to ask you anything they want, which is something you would rather not experience. Try to stack the deck in your favor as much as you can. Just remember that doing research doesn't guarantee that your committee members won't ask you something else, just that you stand a better chance of directing them.

To study for the oral exam, the first task you should undertake is to research the questions you were asked on the written exam. As soon as you finish the written exam, write down the questions on a separate piece of paper so you don't forget what they were later. In a notebook, either add supplemental information or change your answers as needed, and then memorize your revised answers. Of course, you want to understand the revised answers too, but in the stressful moments of the oral exam, it's better and simply easier to have the answers memorized and ready for your explanations.

Don't forget about the questions just because the written part of the exam is over. If there are any holes in your answers, the first thing your committee will do during the oral exam is try to expose those holes, so have your answers ready. After you have thoroughly researched the written questions, spend time with someone else who has knowledge of your discipline and request that he or she test your ability to think on the spot. Just as law students do mock trials, you should practice mock exams. While you can likely memorize the facts on your own, it's extremely difficult (if not impossible) to learn how to think on your own. Just like any other skill, thinking needs to be rehearsed. Having someone around trying to "throw you off" by taking you in different, unexpected directions will help immensely in learning how to keep your cool and focus on the question being asked.

WHAT DOES PLAYING BASEBALL HAVE TO DO WITH A PhD?

When I was a teenager, my mother used to play catch with me in the backyard. An accomplished softball player in her youth, she knew that the best way to train my baseball skills was to throw the ball in a direction different from where she was looking: sometimes as a grounder, sometimes as a fly ball, sometimes to my left, sometimes to my right. I never knew where the ball was going, and thus, I had to learn how to react. These "training sessions" in our backyard were tough because I was always moving, always thinking, always trying to anticipate. This is what you need to do to successfully study for your comps. Find someone who can push your mind in different directions.

Ask your advisor if he or she will help you practice for the oral exam by throwing questions at you. Some advisors won't help you because they (wrongly) think that you should stand on your own for the exam without any "coaching." As a coach, however, I've never once expected my athletes to run a race without me first preparing them. After I had changed advisors (for the second time), I found out that my dissertation advisor met with his students after their written exams to review their responses before their oral exams. To my surprise, it was a much more supportive and learning process for the students at this other university.

"PAPER PhD"

Much like the content of the qualifying exam, not all exam protocols are the same. The exact nature of your exam process will be
dictated largely by the philosophy of your advisor. Some advisors
and departments view the qualifying exam as the doctoral student's
first chance to prove him or herself. Consequently, they take the
qualifying exam very seriously. They immediately throw you into
the deep end of the pool and test whether you can swim on your
own. On the other hand, some advisors and departments view the
PhD process more as an apprenticeship—you're there to learn from
others who will help you grow into a scholar. Both approaches
have their advantages and disadvantages. For example, this latter
approach, if not controlled, can lead to babying the students and
produce what I call "paper PhDs." You may have received the
piece of paper that says you have earned your PhD, but since you
never stood on your own to get it, you don't have the tools to
succeed when you're on your own in the real world as a faculty
member and researcher. You certainly don't want a paper PhD,
but you also don't want to drown in the deep end. Again, this all
goes back to the choices you make when choosing your school and
advisor, so choose wisely.

CHAPTER 6

The Dissertation

"If you want to make a new contribution, you've got to make a whole new preparation."
—STEPHEN COVEY, PhD

Congratulations on getting this far. You have now become what is referred to as an ABD—All But Dissertation—but don't get too excited yet. Although the dissertation is the final hurdle between you and your diploma, it's quite a big hurdle.

By the time you get to the dissertation—the dreaded event for some doctoral students and the pièce de résistance for others—you've likely already spent three to four (and sometimes more) years on your degree, taking classes, pursuing other research, writing manuscripts, and preparing for your qualifying exam. You're already exhausted, and there's still the dissertation. If students drop out of their doctoral programs (which often happens), it's almost always during the dissertation process.

The dissertation is the project and the process that marks your transition from student to scholar. To a large extent, it defines the doctoral process and will consequently define your PhD. As the seminal work and right of passage of your PhD degree, the dissertation is not about doing the least amount of work possible in order to complete the degree; it's not about simply trying to win the approval of your committee, either. Instead, it's about trying to write something that you can proudly show scholars and say, "This is my work. This is who I am. This is the very best I can do."

The dissertation is unique from any other project or assignment you've done while in school, and that's where the problem lies for many students. There's a major discrepancy between the criteria by which students are admitted to doctoral programs and the criteria by which they're awarded their PhD degree. To be admitted to a doctoral program, you must have been a good course taker; to earn your PhD, however, you have to stand on your own feet as an independent researcher and make an original and significant contribution to knowledge. Thus, once you're in a doctoral program, you're asked and expected to do things you have never done before.

Although many doctoral students begin to apply for jobs when they are an ABD, I believe it's better to finish what you've started before entering the "real world." If you already have one hand in the job pool, it's going to become that much more difficult to focus on what you've spent the last three to four years in school trying to achieve, namely earning the coveted PhD degree. Many students even begin jobs when they are still an ABD, as many universities and private companies will accept ABD applicants; but many of those students never finish their PhDs as a result. Even without a job, it's hard to finish—at least half of the ABDs quit before finishing—so finish the degree, then find a job.

Many students think they need to do something groundbreaking or revolutionary for their dissertations. You don't. However, it *is* expected that you contribute something significant to the body of literature. As you go through the dissertation process, you'll find that your committee's opinions of your dissertation and of you are highly subjective. But if there's one objective side to your committee's opinions, if there's one standard that they use, it's that your dissertation must be an original and significant addition to the current body of literature in your discipline; so choose your topic and execution carefully.

Having said that, your dissertation doesn't necessarily have to become your magnum opus (although many people will view it that way), and whatever you do, don't try to win a Nobel or Pulitzer Prize for your dissertation. Only a few people in history have won a Nobel Prize for their doctoral work, and unless you're incredibly brilliant, clever, lucky, and work in one of the few areas in which they award Nobel Prizes, you're not likely to win one. You can cure cancer, develop a plan for world peace, or write the next great piece of literature after you finish your PhD; but for now at least, be content that you've come this far, and work with your advisor to make your dissertation manageable and something that you can complete in a reasonable amount of time.

There's an unwritten rule in science that if you start an experiment, you should be alive when the experiment is finished. Of course, they don't tell you that in graduate school. As my friend's father (who has an EdD) used to say, "The best dissertation is a signed one."

At most schools, you will not be given free rein to choose the topic of your dissertation. More often than not, you'll be asked to follow a line of research that your advisor wants or research that is connected to a grant. However, if you listened to the advice in Chapter 1 and chose the right school because you found a match between your research interests and those of your advisor—you won't believe how often people don't follow this simple advice—then you're not likely to get stuck doing research for your dissertation in which you don't have any vested interest.

If you're in a scientific discipline, the dissertation will likely be an extension of the line of research that has been carried out by your advisor and his or her former students. This makes things easier for you, since you won't have to reinvent the wheel; former students will have already paved your way. If you're in a liberal arts discipline or one that is multidisciplinary, you'll likely have more freedom in choosing your topic. My friend studying communication and culture said, "I had complete freedom in choosing my topic. When the final proposal was approved, my advisor told me that X and Y must be included in the dissertation, but in general, I had complete control over what I was going to research and argue. I followed the line of research of my advisor insofar as I was influenced by a lot of the same cultural and rhetorical theorists that he used in his own work, but it was more of an influence over a way of thinking than over my specific project."

Speak to your advisor about your dissertation as soon as you can after starting your degree. The sooner you know what your dissertation will entail, the sooner you can start collecting information and the smoother the overall process will be, as you can work on parts of the proposal well in advance while you're still taking classes.

CHANGING DISSERTATIONS

One day, shortly after passing my qualifying exam, I was sitting in my advisor's office when he said to me, "Jason, I have something to tell you that you may struggle with. I think you should change your dissertation topic." My head, which was already exhausted from the previous year's work, started spinning. Having to change your dissertation topic after you've already written and revised a sixty-three-page proposal and planned out your entire research project, including purchasing equipment and supplies, learning how to use computer programs to process your data, arranging your experimental setup, and pilot testing a few subjects, is another example of how not to earn your PhD degree.

Once you know the exact topic of your dissertation, your committee will expect some things from you (e.g., literature review, hypotheses, statistical procedures, main arguments, and many others), which you should write into your proposal and prepare to talk about during the proposal defense. For example, understand how your study adds to the body of literature. Understand the prior research and which specific studies are crucial to your study. Understand the limitations of your research—the ability to generalize about populations different from your sample and the inability to control for confounding variables are big ones. Understand the statistical aspects of your research. What statistical tests will you use to analyze your data?

Give yourself at least one to two years to complete your dissertation, and always assume there will come bumps, if not gaping potholes, along the way. During times of stress—and there will be stress—it's helpful to talk to others who are dealing with the same issues as you. Go out with the other students in your department for a beer on Friday nights to vent. If the stress really gets severe, or if you simply cannot find ways to motivate yourself to get through the dissertation, many schools offer a dissertation support group for students going through similar difficulties with their dissertations.

WRITING THE PROPOSAL AND DISSERTATION

Most people have a difficult time articulating their thoughts in print. Eloquence aside, most people have a hard time simply being clear and concise. This may be especially true for people in scientific disciplines because science and writing don't mix well. Ever wonder why textbooks, especially scientific textbooks, are so boring to read? The two activities use different parts of your brain. The left side of your brain is typically used for math and analytical thinking, while the right side is primarily used for art, language, and writing. Most people are either right- or left-brain dominant, and consequently, I've come across very few scientists who have also been excellent writers.

If you're one of those left-brained people who have trouble writing, you have a long road ahead of you because there is tons of writing involved in earning a PhD. If you're working in a liberal arts or fine arts discipline, you likely already have some writing skills. If writing still gives you trouble, most universities have writing centers or tutors who can edit your writing; or you can always hire a professional writer to help you. It's unfortunate that most doctoral programs don't spend enough time dealing with the quality of students' writing or even offer a dissertation writing course for their students. Though you may not need those writing skills to barrel through your dissertation, you may end up utilizing them the rest of your career, especially if you choose to become a college professor and hope to publish articles in your discipline. Writing being such an integral component of research, all doctoral programs, regardless of discipline, should offer a writing course of their own or require students to take a writing course in the English department. If you want to become a successful scholar, the ability to write (and write well) is absolutely necessary. When you submit your dissertation proposal or the final version of your dissertation, your committee will have a hard time getting to the ideas you present if they can't get past the bad writing.

Becoming a Writer

The best way to write your proposal and dissertation is to block out times during the day specifically reserved for writing. You can't write something this large and involved by writing fifteen minutes here and another thirty minutes there. Novelists and playwrights don't write that way, and neither should you. Make an appointment with yourself to write. Don't wait for inspiration.

Of course, that doesn't mean you should ignore those moments when inspiration strikes. It's always helpful to have some paper and a pencil handy so that you can write things down as you think of them. Don't rely on your memory because you may easily forget later. I used to lay awake at night thinking about things before I fell asleep. I bet there aren't too many people in the world losing sleep over issues concerning the endurance physiology of elite distance runners, just as there weren't back when I was working on my PhD degree! Sometimes, those moments of inspiration come when you are actually in front of your computer, working on your manuscript. Those are the best moments—when the words fly out of your head faster than you can type them, and the manuscript seems to just write itself. Admittedly, those moments are rare. Most of the time, writing is work, and good writing takes time; so don't rely on inspiration to get you through your proposal and dissertation.

For me, writing has always been my strength as a student—I started working as a professional freelance writer before I began my PhD and continued writing during my time in school—however, this fact didn't prevent my advisor from requiring that I revise my manuscript multiple times before ever handing it to him. While in school, I split my writing time between my dissertation and national consumer magazines. I even started writing this book while still working on my degree. Perhaps the hardest part for me to accept about writing the dissertation was writing all those pages and not getting paid for the privilege! That's not to say that writing isn't work. There are plenty of times that my writing is slow. Sometimes, I have no idea what I want to say! Similarly, I get the sense that this is true for other writers as well—a quick trip to the local bookstore can reveal that there's a great deal of fluff contained within many nonfiction books. Even the best writers in the world would agree that they have to work to refine and maintain their craft, so don't get frustrated.

When you're writing, don't let things (or other people) become distractions. Admittedly, this is hard to do at times. You'd be surprised at how easily your mind can start to wander. One minute you're having a great thought about existentialism, and the next minute you're wondering how to get the phone number of the attractive student in your existentialism class. I've met countless students who've had terrible trouble motivating themselves to write and get their thoughts onto the page. However, if you force yourself to write, preferably at the same time every day, it'll become easier as you train yourself to "turn on" your writing skills on a regular basis. Treat the dissertation as you would your job, but treat it as though it's your muse, too. And think of yourself as a writer. Keeping ideas in your head doesn't make you a writer; writing does.

If you have trouble writing full paragraphs or even full sentences that articulate your thoughts, then start with your notes. Spend time taking notes on the literature you've read and try connecting those notes together. You can always create full sentences and paragraphs later. The important thing is to get some of your initial thoughts down on paper or inputted in the computer, no matter how rough or inarticulate they may sound at first.

When you can't seem to wrap your head around an idea or maybe you have writer's block, try writing down what the problem is (like a diagnosis) or speaking about the problem into a tape recorder (like a researcher or physician would). Talk the problem over with yourself. Sometimes, addressing the problem itself can help get you through the rough patches. If this still doesn't work, then consider going for a run or walking your dog. Often, you'll notice that by taking a step back and not thinking about something, your brain will relax and become more open and responsive to new perspectives and ideas. Some of my greatest, most insightful thoughts have occurred to me during the quiet, peaceful moments immediately after a run when my brain is clear to think and write. In fact, a number of studies have shown that exercise reduces stress and improves cognitive functioning. Scientists believe that exercise enhances the formation and survival of new nerve cells in the brain while also enhancing the connections between preexisting nerve cells. So what better time to exercise than when you're working on your doctoral dissertation?

When you write, find a place that is quiet and comfortable so you can focus solely on your writing. Maybe that means creating a home office, going to the library with your laptop computer, or sitting at Starbucks with a latté. I've spent most of my time writing in my home office, escaping every once in a while to Starbucks for their mocha Frappuccinos and the occasional conversation with an attractive coed—Starbucks may not be the best place for me to actually get work done. Once or twice, I took my laptop over to the law school library to get a glimpse of how the other half lives; and even when I moved across the country to complete my dissertation under a different advisor, I snuck into a secluded and exclusive resort outside of town to write in view of the mountains (and to use their water slide by the pool). While sometimes it's helpful to immerse yourself in your familiar environment—like the graduate student office, among other grad students in your discipline—other times it's helpful to immerse yourself in a completely foreign environment. Wherever you choose to write, make sure you have a comfortable chair to sit on because you'll be sitting there for long stretches of time.

Procrastination

There seems to be a stereotype among those both inside and outside of academia that graduate students are procrastinators. Part of this stereotype may come from the fact that things become very open-ended at the dissertation point of your degree. There are no set timelines, only those self-imposed. Although universities may set a limit on the amount of time between passing your qualifying exam and defending your dissertation, that limit is relaxed. In fact, at my university, it was seven years! Remember, you graduate only after you have successfully defended your dissertation and submitted all the required paperwork and copies of your dissertation to the university graduate school. That said, the open-ended nature of the PhD degree can quickly become a disaster waiting to happen.

When you talk to your peers, it will seem as if everyone's dissertation is "a work in progress." Doctoral students are notorious for complaining about their dissertations. Sometimes, you may feel that it's never going to get done, but that's normal. I felt that many times, and I knew many others who felt exactly the same way. Although the dissertation can be a bear at times, don't let it get you down, and don't look for things to divert your attention. The only way it will ever get done is if you simply work hard and complete it. Just take it one step at a time. While it is okay to take some planned breaks from the hard, and sometimes tedious, work once in a while, lying on your couch and watching Oprah or Dr. Phil in the middle of the afternoon when you should be working on the next chapter of your dissertation is yet another example of how not to earn your PhD degree. And just for the record, Dr. Phil earned his PhD in organizational psychology long before he met Oprah and became famous.

If you do procrastinate, ask yourself why you do so. Is it because you feel you're not a good writer and therefore shy away from the task? Is it because sometimes you don't feel like putting forth the effort? Admittedly, it's much easier to lie on your couch and watch mindless TV or frequent the bars with your friends than it is to think hard about your dissertation. At these moments, set small goals for yourself. Don't think about the entire dissertation. Instead, focus on one page, maybe even one paragraph at a time. Tell yourself that you're not going to get out of your chair until that one page or one paragraph is done. If you can work through just one thought or write one page a day, then you'll have worked through ten thoughts or written ten pages after ten days—and that's a lot of progress.

Dissertation Format

Once completed, the proposal becomes the first three chapters of a scientific dissertation: (1) Introduction (with Purpose and Hypotheses as the final sections of the Introduction), (2) Literature Review, and (3) Methodology (this latter chapter, in addition to the purpose and hypotheses, only pertains to those whose research involves doing an experiment). The remaining chapters that define the scientific dissertation are: (4) Results, (5) Discussion, and (6) Conclusion (and since the Conclusion is often only one or two pages, you can make it the last section of your Discussion chapter rather than have it be its own chapter). In addition to those basic chapters, there's also the front matter (e.g., committee acceptance page, acknowledgments, preface, dedication, abstract, table of contents, and lists of tables and figures) and any raw data or forms you want to include as appendices. Scientific dissertations can also be qualitative rather than quantitative. For example, disciplines in education (e.g., primary and secondary education, educational psychology, and special education, among others) often use interviews and questionnaires as their data, with the dissertation still using the preset chapters previously described.

Nonscientific dissertations can take on a number of formats, as they conform less to preset chapters than scientific ones. The chapters, each of which may have a different focus, are more of your own choosing, like those in a book. As my friend who was earning his PhD in rhetoric in the department of communication and culture explained to me, the structure is of the student's choosing based on the specific dissertation topic and how one best feels the topic can (and should) be approached. Interested in race and racism, my friend was writing his dissertation on the rhetoric of racial comedy. His dissertation, he told me, could be divided into the following chapters: Introduction, followed by a few chapters analyzing specific comedic texts, including African American comedians Dave Chappelle and Chris Rock as well as Asian comedian Margaret Cho. Chapters could also be divided based on genre. For example, one chapter could address television sitcoms, one might cover stand-up comedians, one may include movies, and so on. Alternatively, chapters could be divided based on different functions of racial comedy. One chapter could deal with how comedy is used as a tool of control and domination to reinforce negative social hierarchies, another chapter could deal with comedy as a tool of social critique and transgression, and another chapter could pull these different roles together. As you can see, there are a number of possibilities.

If you're in a scientific discipline, you'll notice that scientific journal articles all sound the same when you read them. It's as if they all could have been written by the same person. That's because scientific writing is very formulaic. While this may make for a boring read at times, it does make writing manuscripts for publication and your dissertation much easier. Unlike writing a magazine article or a book, there's a lot of redundancy in a dissertation. You state something, restate it in another section or chapter, and then restate it again later. To get a sense of the style, tone, and format, read the recent dissertations of your advisor's former students. You can either find the dissertations in the library or ask your advisor if you may borrow his or her copy—advisors always get a copy of their students' dissertations. This will help you immensely when writing your dissertation, especially if your research is an extension of a former student's.

Together, all of your chapters can total over a hundred to two hundred pages. Don't be daunted by that figure—if you work on one chapter at a time, you'd be surprised at how quickly the pages add up. There's no required page length for a dissertation. Say what you need to say without digressing into areas that are not pertinent to your research project. At the same time, be thorough. While some dissertations can reach their conclusion in seventy-five pages, others may take more than two hundred. I've personally seen dissertations as short as thirty-five pages and others as long as three hundred. Just remember, poor dissertations are generally notable for what is omitted rather than what is included.

THE CHAPTERS OF THE DISSERTATION

To make the writing of your dissertation proposal (and subsequent dissertation) a bit less stressful, I've included the following advice on each of the chapters, each section accompanied by brief examples of what not to do and followed by examples of what to do. (Note that the example paragraphs do not all come from the same research study or dissertation topic). Since scientific dissertations have a specific structure to them, I've included examples of each section (Introduction, Purpose, Hypotheses, Literature Review, Methodology, Data Analysis, Limitations, Results, Discussion, and Conclusions). Dissertations in the liberal arts and humanities are typically written with a more narrative style without preset delineated chapters. The only preset chapters of a nonscientific dissertation are: Introduction and Literature Review. The organization and titles of other chapters and sections are largely decided by you and are based on your exact topic, what makes sense to present within your argument, and the answers to your research question.

Introduction

Although the Introduction is the first chapter of both the scientific and nonscientific dissertation, appearing immediately following the front matter (Title Page, Signature Page, Copyright Page, Acknowledgments, Abstract, Table of Contents, List of Tables, and List of Figures if a scientific dissertation), write the Introduction after the Literature Review chapter. The Introduction is an overview of your research or your dissertation topic, including a brief summary of your Literature Review. As with any piece of writing, the Introduction sets the tone of your body of work, and it serves as your opportunity to grab the reader's attention. If you have a creative side, the Introduction is a great place to show it—although be careful with your Introduction if you're writing a scientific dissertation, since your committee members, especially if they're old school types, may shun any attempt at creative or narrative writing. Begin the Introduction from a wide perspective and finish with a narrow one, including why your specific research project or topic is important and what specific question(s) you hope to answer. At the end of the Introduction, state your purpose and hypotheses (if you're conducting an experiment), using a separate subheading for each. Your hypotheses should include statements about each dependent (outcome) variable that you intend to measure. For a nonscientific dissertation, clearly state your thesis statement at the end of the Introduction.

EXAMPLE OF HOW *NOT* TO WRITE
YOUR INTRODUCTION:

A pattern exists between breathing and stride rate in animals and humans.★ This pattern does not seem to be preset, as many of the studies have shown it to be infrequent or dependent on other factors.★ All of the studies examining the pattern between breathing and stride rate have used submaximal speeds and unfit or moderately fit subjects. Whether a pattern between breathing and stride rate exists in highly trained endurance athletes during intense exercise remains to be examined. Examining how breathing and running mechanics are coordinated (i.e., entrained) in elite distance runners during intense exercise may shed light on the influences of breathing in this unique population.

EXAMPLE OF HOW TO WRITE
YOUR INTRODUCTION:

There is considerable evidence that a pattern exists between breathing and stride rate in animals★ and humans,★ specifically that the stride rhythm imposes its pattern or entrains the pattern of breathing. However, this pattern does not seem to be preset, as many of the studies on humans have shown it to be infrequent or dependent on other factors, such as fitness level.★ Furthermore, all of the studies examining the pattern between breathing and stride rate have done so using submaximal speeds and unfit or moderately fit subjects. Whether a pattern between these two variables still exists in highly trained endurance athletes during steady-state and non-steady-state exercise remains to be examined.

Endurance athletes are a peculiar breed of human. There are a number of characteristics that separate them from their less fit counterparts, including a large cardiac output, a large and intricate capillary network perfusing the skeletal muscles, lots of red blood cells and hemoglobin to carry oxygen, and an abundance of oxygen-consuming mitochondria, all leading to a high rate of oxygen consumption. Sometimes, the level of work that these athletes can do places too high of a demand on the cardiopulmonary system to supply the necessary oxygen to sustain the work. Ironically, this leads to these endurance athletes experiencing some of the same consequences during exercise as individuals with cardiopulmonary disease. For instance, many endurance athletes exhibit a decrease in the arterial partial pressure of oxygen during maximal exercise, resulting in a desaturation of oxygen from hemoglobin, a condition given the inauspicious name "exercise-induced hypoxemia."* Additionally, many of these athletes reach the lungs' mechanical limit of generating airflow during intense exercise and are said to be "flow-limited" because they cannot breathe enough to match their high metabolic demand, leading to an inadequate pulmonary gas exchange.* Thus, while pulmonary performance is not considered to limit endurance exercise performance in healthy, but unfit, individuals, it possibly can in elite endurance athletes, as it does in individuals with pulmonary disease, but for vastly different reasons.

Examining how breathing and running mechanics are coordinated (i.e., entrained) in elite distance runners during intense exercise may help to answer both an applied science question, such as how elite athletes optimize their ventilation while running at different speeds, and a pure biological question, such as how the lungs are designed to work during locomotion. Of particular interest is whether the entrainment of breathing frequency to stride rate occurs during intense exercise in the face of cardiorespiratory and pulmonary limitations that are curiously imposed upon the elite endurance athlete as a result of his or her remarkable, if not envious, ability to achieve and sustain high workloads, such as exercise-induced hypoxemia and expiratory flow limitation.

* References have been omitted, but would normally be included where the asterisks are placed.

Note how the second example includes more detail than the first. It addresses the characteristics of elite endurance athletes and makes a stronger argument for why these athletes should be studied as well as what exactly can be learned from studying them.

Purpose

The Purpose, as you might guess, is a very important part of the scientific dissertation proposal. Not only does it state to your committee exactly what it is that you plan to address, it also states the purpose to yourself. Think of it like creating a business plan: once you know exactly what it is that you're trying to accomplish, actually accomplishing your goal becomes significantly easier.

While working on my degree, people asked me all the time what I was doing for my dissertation. After writing a clear purpose statement, it was easy for me to answer them rather than fumble all over myself trying to explain, as I had before. More importantly, it was easier for me to answer that question for myself.

Your purpose statement should be one paragraph, in which you describe (or list) the purpose(s) of your proposed research study. The purpose should be clear and concise. The more clear and concise it is, the easier it will be for you to design an experiment around it. While it may seem easier to detail many purposes, too many will make your study overwhelming. Discuss with your advisor what exactly it is that you want to find out from your experiment. As the cliché goes, don't bite off more than you can chew.

EXAMPLE OF HOW *NOT* TO WRITE YOUR PURPOSE:

The purpose of this study is to compare the effects of different drugs on blood pressure.

EXAMPLE OF HOW TO WRITE YOUR PURPOSE:

The purpose of this study is to compare the effects of two blood pressure–lowering drugs—Lopramine and Carpimil*—on average resting blood pressure in patients with hypertension (defined as a resting blood pressure greater than 160/90 obtained on more than two occasions within one week) for 24 and 48 hours following drug administration.

* Drug names are not real.

Notice the detail of the second example—it states exactly which drugs will be compared (Lopramine and Carpimil), the population that will be examined (patients with hypertension), the dependent variable (average resting blood pressure), and when the data will be collected (24 and 48 hours following drug administration). All of this detail is important because each one of these things can affect the outcome of the study.

Hypotheses

Each Purpose you state should also have a Hypothesis associated with it. If the purpose of your study is to examine the relationship of cigarette smoking on the incidence of lung cancer, your hypothesis obviously can't be that cigarette smoking causes lung cancer, not unless you're somehow measuring the carcinogenic effects of cigarettes. From this purpose statement, all you can say is that there either is or is not a statistically significant relationship between cigarette smoking and the incidence of lung cancer. If your study shows that there is a high correlation between cigarette smoking and the incidence of lung cancer, cigarette smoking may or may not be the cause of the lung cancer. Remember, there still may be other characteristics of people who smoke that can be linked to the development of lung cancer.

The Hypotheses section can be written simply as a list of educated guesses about what you believe your results will show. However, those educated guesses should be directed by previous research, and it may significantly help to include a research-based rationale after each hypothesis. As a result, you'll need to become very familiar with the findings reported in the literature before writing this section, yet another reason why you should write the entire Introduction, with Purpose and Hypotheses, after you have written the Literature Review. Each Hypothesis should be testable from a statistical perspective. You don't want to end up with hypotheses that cannot be tested, after all.

EXAMPLE OF HOW *NOT* TO WRITE YOUR HYPOTHESES:

The hypothesis of this study is that Lopramine will be better than Carpimil.

It is hypothesized that there will be a difference in average resting blood pressure between Lopramine and Carpimil.

EXAMPLE OF HOW TO WRITE YOUR HYPOTHESES:

The hypotheses of this study include: (1) Average resting blood pressure will be significantly lower after the administration of Lopramine compared to after the administration of Carpimil 24 hours following drug administration, and (2) Average resting blood pressure will be significantly lower after the administration of Carpimil compared to after the administration of Lopramine 48 hours following drug administration.

Note the direction given to the hypothesized differences in the above example. While saying that one drug will be better than another also gives direction, it is not as specific as saying that one drug will result in a lower or higher blood pressure. Stating a direction of the expected difference is also a matter of statistics, with the use of the word "significant" or "significantly" meaning that the difference is statistically different. When you test for a difference between two interventions, but you don't know the direction of that difference (i.e., you don't know which intervention will be better), you must use a two-tailed statistical test; but when you test for a difference in a specific direction between two interventions (i.e., you hypothesize which intervention will have a higher or lower result), you can use a one-tailed statistical test, which is a more powerful test, provided that the study's result is in the direction you hypothesized. And a more powerful test means that you are better able to detect a significant (statistical) difference between interventions or groups, if indeed there is one.

Literature Review

All dissertations, scientific or nonscientific, regardless of the specific discipline of study, include some kind of review of the literature. Your review should begin as an initial survey of articles related to your research topic and then move toward a more critical review of the most pertinent work. The Literature Review is not a summary of articles or essays. It's not a "report" on the state of your academic discipline or even of your specific dissertation topic. It's actually a scholarly analysis and synthesis of information and research findings that lead your reader (and you) to your proposed research question. Think of it as a search for the hole in a specific topic that you plan to fill with your own research.

Write the Literature Review chapter first. It will be easier to go back and write the Introduction after you have a strong sense of the literature and where it's leading you with your own research.

Of course, to write the Literature Review chapter, you must first review the literature in your subject area.

SCIENTIFIC DISCIPLINES

If your dissertation is in a scientific discipline, find as many journal articles as you can on your dissertation topic—ideally, you're supposed to find them all. Read them and highlight the important findings, the methods employed, as well as the number and characteristics of subjects. On a separate piece of paper, make a list (or a table) of all the studies, the number and characteristics of their subjects, their interventions, and their findings. Categorize the studies based on their findings so it will be easier for you to refer to them in your chapter. After you have collected and read all the articles, you can begin writing the Literature Review chapter. Use the table of studies you have created as a "cheat sheet" to help you write this chapter. To make your Literature Review chapter more sophisticated (and impress your committee), you may want to include a formal table of studies that summarizes the findings of the pertinent literature.

Your Literature Review will also help you design your study and write your Methodology section, which will be addressed later. First, try to understand why the researchers performed their studies the way they did and if there are any flaws in their methodologies. Review the questions in Chapter 2 on thinking critically.

Often, there are conflicting results between different scientific studies in the literature, primarily because the results of any study are only the results of how the study was performed; no two studies are ever done exactly the same way, under the same conditions. If you are doing your dissertation in an area where there are some conflicting results among studies, it's always helpful to try to figure out why that conflict or disagreement exists. Then, you can write about it so your advisor and your committee both know that you've read all the literature. While writing your Literature Review chapter, here are some key questions to ask yourself:

- What did each study find?
- How many subjects did each study include?
- What are some of the details of each study's methodology?
- What are the details of each experimental condition?
- Can you decipher the reasons for any conflicting results between studies?
- Should all of the studies be given equal weight? If not, why not?
- What are some major flaws of the studies?
- Taking all of the studies into account, what are the salient conclusions? What are the take-home messages?

EXAMPLE OF HOW *NOT* TO WRITE YOUR LITERATURE REVIEW:

Some studies have shown protein ingestion along with carbohydrate hastens the rate of glycogen resynthesis and improves endurance performance,★ while other studies have reported no benefit with the simultaneous ingestion of protein.★ Differences in findings may be due to methodological differences between studies.

EXAMPLE OF HOW TO WRITE YOUR LITERATURE REVIEW:

Research that has examined protein ingestion along with carbohydrate on the rate of glycogen resynthesis or endurance performance (Table 1) has yielded inconsistent results, as some studies have shown this strategy to hasten the rate of glycogen resynthesis and improve endurance performance, especially when the amount of carbohydrate ingested is less than that recommended for maximal glycogen resynthesis,★ while other studies have reported no benefit with the simultaneous ingestion of protein.★ Roy and Tarnopolsky (1998) also reported this latter result following resistance exercise. At least some of the discrepancy in the literature may be attributed to the use of beverages that were either not isocaloric★ or contained different amounts of carbohydrate.★ It is possible that Carrithers et al. (2000) and Tarnopolsky et al. (1997) did not observe differences in muscle glycogen content between the treatments because the carbohydrate-protein beverages contained less carbohydrate than the carbohydrate-only beverages (0.7 vs. 1.0 g/kg/hr and 0.75 vs. 1.0 g/kg/hr, respectively). In the study of Rotman et al. (2000), both the carbohydrate and carbohydrate-protein beverages already contained the recommended amount of carbohydrate for maximal glycogen resynthesis (0.85 and 0.6 g/kg/hr, respectively), which may have obscured any added benefit of protein.

The specific type of carbohydrate contained in the beverages has also varied between studies. Two studies used an equal mix of glucose and sucrose in both their carbohydrate and carbohydrate-protein beverages,★ one study used sucrose,★ one used a mix of dextrose and maltodextrin,★ one used an equal mix of glucose and maltodextrin,★ and one used a mix of sucrose and maltodextrin.★ Carrithers et al. (2000) did not even use the same type of carbohydrate between the different treatment beverages, as their carbohydrate-only beverage contained glucose while their carbohydrate-protein beverage contained fructose and dextrose. All three studies that reported a beneficial effect of combining carbohydrate with protein★ used maltodextrin, a complex carbohydrate, as one of the carbohydrate ingredients. Of the studies that reported no additional benefit with the co-ingestion of protein,★ three used sucrose★ and three used glucose★ as one of the carbohydrate ingredients. Despite some similarities in the type(s) of carbohydrate used between studies with similar findings, the type of carbohydrate used does not help explain the contrasting results in the literature.

Another potential reason for the conflicting results may be due to differences in the frequency of supplementation. For example, studies finding a beneficial effect with the co-ingestion of protein have most often used feeding intervals of two hours,★ while studies reporting no benefit with the co-ingestion of protein have most often used feeding intervals of less than one hour★ (Table 1). It appears, therefore, that both a high carbohydrate content of the beverage (enough to meet the recommendation for maximal glycogen resynthesis) and the more frequent ingestion of carbohydrate negate any benefit of added protein. The only thing that seems to be clear, obvious as it may be, is that beverages containing carbohydrate or carbohydrate plus protein are more effective than plain water or a placebo at lengthening time to exhaustion during exercise and restoring glycogen after exercise.★

★ References have been omitted, but would normally be included where the asterisks are placed.

Note the pattern that is employed in the second example: the findings of the literature are first summarized, followed by a discussion of why the results between studies are conflicting. Some of the specific numbers from other studies are included in parentheses so the reader can see the differences between studies rather than simply trust your judgment. Using parenthetical data when discussing other studies is a great way to include a few specifics about each study without taking up too much room or digressing. If there are no conflicting results in the area about which you're writing, simply summarize the results and then discuss a couple of representative studies in more detail. Either way, make sure to use the phrase "For example..." a great deal.

NONSCIENTIFIC DISCIPLINES

If your dissertation is in a nonscientific discipline, the Literature Review should be a bit different. You will likely have a wider array of sources, including essays, textbooks, newspaper articles, audio transcripts, visual recordings, microfilm, among others. Collect information regarding the analyses of works related to your thesis, and find arguments or philosophies about your topic. Summarize and synthesize the arguments and ideas of others. Then, identify the conceptual strengths and weaknesses of the existing research, and discuss the gaps that your research will fill. Depending on your exact research question, your Literature Review chapter can take on a number of different slants. For example, say you're researching the portrayal of race in art. Your literature review can focus on cultural differences between the portrayal of race in American, French, and Spanish artwork, or the review can focus on the economic impact of how race is portrayed in American art only. The former slant would require you to find sources that speak to the cultural differences between the three countries as they pertain to the portrayal of race, while the latter slant would require you to find sources that speak to the economic impact of how race is portrayed.

Methodology

If you're in a scientific discipline, the Methodology chapter follows immediately after the Literature Review chapter. Unless you are doing an experiment for which you are developing a unique procedure, use the methods that have already been employed by other researchers in your discipline and dictated by your Literature Review. You don't have to reinvent the wheel. If your research is an extension of a former student's in your department and uses the same or similar methods, ask your advisor for a copy of that student's dissertation so that you can see what methods have been employed before. Although you don't want to restate things verbatim and plagiarize another writer, there's only so many ways to state the technique and method that was employed. Since the Methodology chapter typically reads like a recipe, it's inevitable that dissertations sound similar to one another.

The first section of the Methodology chapter, which is usually given the subheading "Subjects," includes information about your subjects (e.g., age, sex, unique characteristics, among others). The next section, usually given the subheading "Experimental Procedures" or "Experimental Protocol," details how exactly your study will be completed. You can divide the procedures or protocol into subsections that describe each part of your study, and then you can name them as you so choose. The last section, usually given the subheading "Data Analysis," describes how you plan to analyze your data, including the statistical procedures you plan to utilize.

As mentioned previously, the Methodology chapter should read like a recipe book; every minute detail about how you plan on completing your study must be included—even the manufacturer's names and product numbers of the equipment and supplies you use should be listed. Never mind the fact that no one else will ever exactly duplicate your study and therefore will never need to know every single detail. The idea is that if they were to duplicate your study, they would be able to do so just by reading what you have written. That said, the most important key to your Methodology chapter is detail.

For your proposal, everything should be written in future tense. "Subjects will be asked to sign an informed consent form," is an example of a phrase you may use in your Methodology chapter. To turn your proposal into your dissertation, simply change all of the future tense verbs to past tense, stating, for example, "Subjects signed an informed consent form."

EXAMPLE OF HOW *NOT* TO WRITE YOUR METHODOLOGY:

Subjects

Twenty healthy, nonsmoking, college-aged males will be recruited for this study. Each subject will be verbally explained the procedures of the study, including the slight risks associated with performing a maximal physical effort, and will be required to sign an informed consent form prior to his participation.

Blood Sampling

Before the exercise bout, a catheter for blood sampling will be inserted into the subject's antecubital vein. Five blood samples will be collected. A drop of blood will also be collected on a microcuvette and immediately analyzed for hemoglobin concentration. The samples for insulin and free fatty acids (FFA) will be centrifuged at 1,000 g (2,700 RPM) for 15 minutes at room temperature to separate the serum from the plasma. The separated serum will then be pipetted into a plastic transfer tube. All vacutainers and transfer tubes will be labeled accordingly and frozen for later assaying. Insulin concentration will be determined using an enzyme immunoassay kit. Glucose, FFA, and lactate concentrations will be determined using enzyme colorimetric assay kits. All blood samples will be analyzed in triplicate.

EXAMPLE OF HOW TO WRITE YOUR METHODOLOGY:

Subjects

Twenty healthy, nonsmoking, college-aged males (under thirty years of age) from the University of X will be recruited for this study. This sample size is based on a statistical power analysis using prior studies from the literature and 80 percent power. For inclusion in the study, subjects must have no history of disease, which will be determined by a health history questionnaire (Appendix A). Each subject will be verbally explained the procedures of the study, including the slight risks associated with performing a maximal physical effort, and will be required to sign an informed consent form prior to his participation. All procedures of this study will be approved by the University of X's Institutional Review Board.

Blood Sampling

Before the exercise bout, a twenty-gauge catheter for blood sampling will be inserted into the subject's antecubital vein and kept patent with periodic flushings (approximately 1 mL) of sterile saline. Each blood sample (5 mL) will be drawn from the catheter via a syringe and divided into two separate vacutainers: one containing sodium fluoride and potassium oxalate as anticoagulants for determination of blood glucose and lactate concentrations and one plain vacutainer for determination of serum insulin and free fatty acid (FFA) concentrations. Blood samples will be collected immediately prior to and upon completion of the exercise bout and after 30 minutes, 2.5 hours, and 4 hours of recovery. A drop of blood will also be collected on a microcuvette and immediately analyzed for hemoglobin concentration using a B-hemoglobin photometer (HemoCue, Ängelholm, Sweden). The samples for insulin and free fatty acids will be centrifuged (Accuspin FR #343440, Beckman Instruments, Palo Alto, CA) at 1,000 g (2,700 RPM) for 15 minutes at room temperature (22–23°C) to separate the serum from the plasma. The separated serum will then be pipetted into a plastic transfer tube. All vacutainers and transfer tubes will be labeled accordingly and frozen for later assaying. Insulin concentration will be determined using an enzyme immunoassay kit (Human Insulin EIA #08-10-1113-01, American Laboratory Products Company, Windham, NH). Glucose, FFA, and lactate concentrations will be determined using enzyme colorimetric assay kits (Glucose C2, Wako Chemicals, Richmond, VA; NEFA C, Wako Chemicals, Richmond, VA; #735-10, Trinity Biotech, St. Louis, MO, respectively). All blood samples will be analyzed in triplicate, with the mean concentration used for data analysis after being corrected for hemoconcentration using each subject's hemoglobin values.

Note the inclusion of details in the second example: when and how much blood will be taken, how the blood will be handled, and the manufacturers' names, locations, and product numbers for all equipment to be used. Also, the sentence "All procedures of this study will be approved by the University of X's Institutional Review Board" must always be included in the Subjects section.

Data Analysis

The Data Analysis section of the Methodology chapter in a scientific dissertation is simple to write, as there are standard procedures to perform certain analyses. You just need to be clear about what it is you want to measure. To know that, review your hypotheses, which will help direct you. For example, to compare the means of two or more sets of data or groups of subjects, you will most often use an analysis of variance (ANOVA). Therefore, many descriptions of data analyses sound the same. When data are collected multiple times on one group of subjects, a repeated measures ANOVA is used.

Moreover, if you only have one dependent variable, you can name it in this section. If you have many dependent variables, you can either name them in this section or simply refer to "data" or "independent variables" (which have been described in an earlier section) as I have done in the example below. If you have more than two groups of subjects or sets of data, you will also need to include a *post hoc* test to determine between which groups the differences occur. If you only have two groups of subjects or sets of data, you do not need to include a statement about using a *post hoc* test, as any statistically significant difference that exists will obviously be between the two groups that you are comparing. That's all the statistics you will get in this book, I promise.

EXAMPLE OF HOW *NOT* TO WRITE YOUR DATA ANALYSIS:

An analysis of variance (ANOVA) will be used to compare data. In the case of a main effect, a *post hoc* test will be used. A correlation will be used to determine the relationship between variables.

EXAMPLE OF HOW TO WRITE YOUR DATA ANALYSIS:

A one-way analysis of variance (ANOVA) will be used to compare data between the three groups using commercially available software (SPSS, Chicago, IL). In the case of a significant main effect, a Tukey's *post hoc* test★ will be used to detect the source of the differences. In addition, Pearson correlational analysis will be used to determine the strength of relationship between each of the independent variables. Statistical significance will be set at $p < 0.05$, with a Bonferroni adjustment made for multiple comparisons.

★Or whichever *post hoc* test you choose.

One grammatical mistake I've seen countless times when writing the word data is the use of "is" or "was" rather than "are" or "were." The word "data" is plural; the singular form of data is datum, which you will probably never use because you'll always have more than one number or piece of data with which to work. While some stylebooks and guides will allow that "data" be used like the word "information," in scientific writing it refers to your numbers and figures and is almost always treated as plural. Writing "The data was compared between groups" rather than "The data were compared between groups" is yet another example of how not to earn your PhD degree.

Limitations

Since no research study is perfect, you should briefly (within a page or two) discuss the limitations of your study. For example, are there limitations to your methodology? Is your research limited to a specific population? You should explore these limitations and any strategies that you plan to use to minimize their impact on your results.

For one of my research projects, the treatment I gave my subjects (beverages containing different nutrients) was single-blind (i.e., the researcher does not know which treatment the subjects are given, but the subjects do know or at least could figure it out easily) rather than double-blind (i.e., neither the researcher nor the subjects know which treatment the subjects are given). The single-blind nature of the study, although unavoidable due to the distinctive tastes of the beverages, was still a limitation, as it can create a bias among the subjects that can influence the results.

The Limitations section is the loosest section of the proposal/dissertation because there is no set format. It's based on your own opinions of the important limiting factors of your research. You don't need to drone on and on about every minute detail that can serve as a limiting factor—despite what some people believe about horoscopes and astrology, chances are that how the stars are aligned on the day you collect your data is not going to impact your results.

EXAMPLE OF HOW *NOT* TO WRITE YOUR LIMITATIONS:

A limitation of this study is the inability to generalize the results to populations different from that of the proposed study. A second limitation of this study is the possible inability to generalize the results obtained by running on a treadmill to track or overground running. A third limitation is the lack of an ability to control for other confounding variables that may affect maximal exercise performance.

EXAMPLE OF HOW TO WRITE YOUR LIMITATIONS:

The following represent limitations of the proposed study:

1. The inability to generalize the results to populations different from that of the proposed study. Since elite endurance athletes exhibit unique cardiopulmonary characteristics, especially when exercising at high intensities, the relationship between breathing and stride frequency may also be unique in this population.

2. The possible inability to generalize the results obtained by running on a treadmill to track or overground running. While no previous studies have reported significant differences in stride mechanics between treadmill and overground running, it has been found that overground running incurs a greater metabolic energy cost compared to treadmill running, particularly at faster speeds.* The greater metabolic cost associated with overground running may alter the relationship between breathing and stride rate from that determined by running on a treadmill.

3. The effects of breathing into a mouthpiece. During the testing of the proposed study, subjects will breathe into a mouthpiece connected to a breathing valve. In addition, nose clips will be used to prevent the subjects from breathing through their noses. This method of breathing, while common in a laboratory setting, differs from what these subjects do in practice, which may alter the ventilatory strategy normally used. The heightened awareness of breathing in a laboratory setting, when subjects know that breathing is being monitored, may cause subjects to consciously or subconsciously alter their breathing patterns.

4. The inability to control for other confounding variables that may affect maximal exercise performance. For example, although the subjects will be told to refrain from intense exercise for 24 hours prior to each experimental trial, whether or not they adhere to this recommendation is outside the control of the study design.

* References have been omitted, but would normally be included where the asterisks are placed.

Although the first example does list most of the limitations, it ignores an explanation of each one. The reader is left with too many questions. Why can't you generalize your results to a different population or running overground? What are the confounding variables that cannot be controlled, and why can't they be controlled? However, all of these questions are answered in the second example. The third limitation discussed (breathing into a mouthpiece) is a limitation that normally would not be included since it is standard research practice. Every time physiologists measure ventilation or whole-body metabolism, subjects breathe through snorkel-like mouthpieces and are prevented from breathing through their noses with nose clips. In truth, some of the newest equipment covers the mouth and nose, allowing for more natural breathing. However, the study referred to in the above example was designed to examine the relationship between breathing and stride rate in elite distance runners to determine if these athletes coordinate the two rhythms. Therefore, the fact that they will be asked to breathe differently in the laboratory compared to how they normally breathe when running overground may significantly affect the relationship being addressed by this study, and thus this represents an important limitation. Be sure to include all aspects of your study that you think have the potential to affect your results.

With the writing of the Limitations section, you have completed your dissertation proposal. See? That wasn't so hard, was it? Just don't forget to compile and format the list of references. Now, let's take a look at the additional chapters you'll need for the dissertation itself.

Results

With the Results chapter, you have begun the writing of your formal dissertation. The Results chapter can be viewed simply as a list of your results written in paragraph form. There is no discussion, analysis, opinion, or commenting on your results—it's just the facts. For some of the detailed data, use tables or graphs, and refer to them in the text rather than listing all the numbers in the text. For data not represented in tables or graphs, include the data in the text. Because you are reporting on your completed study, all verbs in the Results and Discussion chapters are in the past tense; and don't forget to now change all of the verbs to past tense in the earlier chapters to officially move from proposal to formal dissertation.

If you're in a scientific discipline with mounds of data to analyze, you will inevitably have to use statistics on the data to obtain the results of your experiment. Although tempting, don't pay someone from the stats department to complete your statistical analyses for you. Unless you can also pay him or her to explain the statistical procedures used in detail, this will only come back to haunt you when you have to defend those statistical procedures in front of your committee, especially if you have someone on your committee who is an expert in statistics. If you're like me and none too fond of stats, you'll have the rest of your research career to pay a statistician to compile the stats for your research after you enter the real world.

EXAMPLE OF HOW *NOT* TO WRITE YOUR RESULTS:

The results of this study showed that time to exhaustion and total work during the endurance performance test were greater when the subjects drank chocolate milk and the fluid-replacement drink compared to when the subjects drank the carbohydrate-replacement drink. There were no differences in heart rate, rating of perceived exertion, blood lactate, body mass, body water, amount of water consumed, pre-exercise diets, and questionnaire responses.

EXAMPLE OF HOW TO WRITE YOUR RESULTS:

Both time to exhaustion and total work performed during the endurance performance test were significantly greater ($p < 0.05$) following ingestion of chocolate milk and the fluid-replacement drink compared to following the carbohydrate-replacement drink (Figure 1). However, there were no significant differences among the three trials in any of the other variables examined in this study, including heart rate (Figure 2) and rating of perceived exertion during the endurance performance trials, and post-exercise blood lactate for the glycogen depletion and endurance performance trials (Table 3). Both body mass and total body water did not differ between treatments or within trials (Table 3). There were no significant differences in the amount of water consumed by the subjects during the recovery period between the chocolate milk, fluid-replacement drink, and carbohydrate-replacement drink trials. In addition, there were no significant differences in the macronutrient composition of the subjects' diets prior to each trial (Table 4) or in the subjects' responses to any of the questions on the questionnaires between trials.

Note the reference to tables and figures (graphs) rather than the listing of all the data within the text. If done well, tables and figures can provide a lot of information while also appealing to the reader. They also take up more pages, making your dissertation seem longer.

It's hard to mess up the writing of the Results chapter, as it is simply a listing of what you found through experimentation. Just remember to be thorough and mention all of your findings. Always write the most important and statistically significant results first, followed by the less important and nonsignificant results.

Match your results statements to your purpose and hypothesis statements from your Introduction chapter—just as each purpose statement has an associated hypothesis, each purpose/hypothesis should have a results statement. For example, if your purpose is to examine the effect of a visual cue on memorization and your hypothesis is that subjects who are given a visual cue will achieve a higher score on a memorization test than subjects who are not given a visual cue, your results section should state either, "Subjects given a visual cue scored significantly higher ($p < 0.05$) on the memorization test than subjects who were not given a visual cue" or "Subjects given a visual cue did not score significantly higher ($p > 0.05$) on the memorization test than subjects who were not given a visual cue." The latter statement can also be written as: "There was no significant difference in memorization test scores between subjects who were given a visual cue and subjects who were not."

If your results do not match your hypotheses, don't attempt to explain why in the Results chapter. Save that for the Discussion chapter, which immediately follows.

Discussion

The Discussion chapter, as you might have already guessed, is where you discuss your results. It is typically the most difficult chapter to write because you need to contextualize your results. If the Results chapter contains "just the facts," then the Discussion attempts to capture "what those facts mean." This includes thoroughly explaining why you found what you found and what that indicates or elucidates about the topic of your dissertation. This chapter requires more critical thinking and interpretation than the others. However, if you remember that dissertation writing in general (and scientific writing in particular) conforms to a formula, then you'll have a much easier time writing your Discussion chapter.

The Discussion chapter follows a basic pattern: you restate your results (without being repetitive); discuss the theory, meaning, and implications behind them; and compare your results to the literature. Discuss your results in the same order as you state them in the Results section, beginning with the most important and the ones that are statistically significant. A dissertation is not like a mystery novel in which you only find out who committed the murder at the end. For your dissertation, tell your reader who the murderer is at the very beginning of the story.

If your results are in contrast to those of other studies, try to explain why. Often—almost too often—researchers pin the difference between study results on the methods. When they don't know why they found something that contrasts with the findings of five other studies, they usually say, "Our results are in contrast to those of Jones et al. (2006), which can be attributed to differences in study design and/or protocol." While the results of any study are largely influenced by how the study was performed, don't rely on this as your only defense unless the difference really can be attributed to different methods. If the methods are different, describe *how* they are different. Give details. If you and Jones et al. (2006) researched how long it required a chicken egg to hatch, and Jones et al. (2006) used an egg incubation temperature of 80 degrees and you incubated the eggs at 100 degrees, make sure you state that difference because that could be the reason why your results differed from Jones et al. (2006), especially if another study found a difference in egg hatching time based on incubation temperature. If such a study exists, you'll definitely need to find and document it since that only strengthens your defense as to why your results differ from any other study.

Follow this pattern of discussion—restating your results; discussing the theory, meaning, and implications behind them; and comparing your results to the literature—for each of your dependent variables, and you'll have a Discussion chapter that will blow your advisor and committee away.

EXAMPLE OF HOW *NOT* TO WRITE YOUR DISCUSSION:

The duration of the contact and noncontact (airborne) phases of the running stride decreased with an increase in running velocity. The subjects in this study increased both stride rate and stride length as velocity increased, with stride length increasing more than stride rate. During all three running speeds, the right heel came in contact with the ground first, followed by the fifth metatarsal, the first metatarsal, and finally the first toe, with the time between these contact points decreasing as speed increased. At the fastest speed, the heel touched down at almost exactly the same instant as the fifth metatarsal.

The electromyographic (EMG) activity showed that the vastus lateralis muscle was activated at three separate times: (1) during the second half of the swing phase, (2) as the knee was extended to reach for the ground, and (3) during the stance phase. The EMG activity for the biceps femoris muscle exhibited a biphasic pattern, especially at a speed of 9.0 mph. This muscle became active following the onset of the vastus lateralis during the second half of the swing phase. The biceps femoris was also active during the stance phase, in conjunction with the increase in activity of the vastus lateralis. The gastrocnemius muscle became active just prior to heel-strike, before the onset of the biceps femoris and vastus lateralis, and remained active until takeoff.

EXAMPLE OF HOW TO WRITE
YOUR DISCUSSION:

As expected, the duration of the contact and noncontact (airborne) phases of the running stride decreased as running velocity increased (Table 1), a finding that is well accepted.★ While both stride rate and stride length increased as velocity increased, stride length increased more than stride rate did. There is considerable evidence to support this finding, as it has been reported that stride rate remains relatively stable when running at submaximal velocities and that a faster velocity is accompanied by a longer stride length.★

During all three running speeds, the right heel (RH) came in contact with the ground first, followed by the fifth metatarsal (R5), the first metatarsal (R1), and finally the first toe (RT), with the time between these contact points decreasing as speed increased (Figures 1–3). This sequence (RH-R5-R1-RT) associated with the foot contact phase is widely accepted as how the foot behaves during distance running, as center of pressure measurements have shown that the center of pressure path initiates laterally and moves medially and anteriorly during the stance phase.★ During distance running, the foot typically lands on the lateral portion of the heel in a slightly supinated and dorsiflexed position, rolls inward (pronates) to absorb the force associated with landing, and finally plantarflexes, pushing off the ground at the first toe. At the fastest speed used in this study (12.6 mph), RH touched down at almost exactly the same instant as R5, suggesting that the subjects landed more toward the midfoot at this faster speed. Runners tend to land farther forward on the foot as running speed increases, especially among elite runners.★

The electromyographic (EMG) activity for the vastus lateralis (VL) muscle exhibited a triphasic activation pattern. This muscle was active during the second half of the swing phase, most likely in conjunction with the flexion of the hip to bring the leg forward. VL again became active as the knee was extended to reach for the ground. Finally, VL was active during the stance phase as the leg was supported on the ground until takeoff. Elliot and Blanksby (1979) reported that the activity of the quadriceps muscles increases during the last half of the swing phase and the initial portion of the support phase. From the magnitude of the EMG signal, the rectified EMG signal, and its linear envelope, it is clear that VL activity increased during the second half of the swing phase and the stance phase (Figures 1–6).

The EMG activity for the biceps femoris (BF) muscle exhibited a distinct biphasic activation pattern, especially at a speed of 9.0 miles per hour (mph) (Figures 1 and 4). This muscle became active following the onset of VL during the second half of the swing phase, during which the knee is being bent as it is brought forward. Figure 8 shows the duration of BF activity for one leg cycle (two consecutive heel strikes). BF was active during the last 26 percent, 24.6 percent, and 29.2 percent of the swing phase at 9.0, 11.0, and 12.6 mph, respectively, with no significant differences between running velocities. This finding is in agreement with the literature, which has reported that the hamstring muscles are active during the latter 25 to 40 percent of the swing phase.* BF was also active during the stance phase, in conjunction with the increase in activity of VL. The hamstrings have been reported to

remain active through the first half of the support phase.★
The interesting finding of co-contraction of the agonist
and antagonist muscles of the thigh is in agreement with
the literature, as it has been reported that the hamstrings
and the quadriceps co-contract to provide stability after
landing.★ The gastrocnemius (GA) muscle became active
just prior to heel-strike, before the onset of BF and VL,
and remained active until takeoff. During midstance
until takeoff, GA is active to plantarflex the foot. This
plantarflexion is then accompanied by hip extension to
drive the leg backward against the ground. Therefore, BF
becomes active to assist the other hip extensor muscles.
The biphasic pattern of BF also occurred during 11.0 and
12.6 mph (Figures 2–5), although the time between the
"offset" of the first peak and the "onset" of the second
peak was shortened due to the shorter duration of foot
contact. Another interesting finding of this study was that
all three muscles were inactive during the initial portion of
the swing phase immediately after takeoff, suggesting that
these muscles do get a recovery period between steps, if
only for a few tenths of a second.

★ References have been omitted, but would normally be included
where the asterisks are placed.

The first example reads more like a restatement of the results,
with no analysis or relationship made to the literature; but these
important aspects are included in the second example. Also note
the use of abbreviations for technical words or terms that are
repeated often. When using abbreviations, make sure you write

out the whole word or term the first time you use it, followed by the abbreviation in parentheses.

Conclusions

I like to think of the Conclusions of the dissertation as the bow with which you wrap the package. It is a brief (one- to two-page) summary of your results, accompanied by their practical implications and applications. You can also use this section to suggest directions for future research on your topic. In fact, you should, since your committee members will be looking for that and may even ask you about your pursuit of this research in the future at your dissertation defense. Suggesting directions for future research shows you have developed a mastery of your research topic and can think like a scientist.

Think of the Conclusions chapter as the "take-home message." What do you want your readers to walk away with? Place your results into a larger context. What do your results suggest about your research topic? Use simple language, and be clear. Be careful not to stretch here—you can't make grandiose statements or conclude something that your results do not allow. For example, if you've found that cultured cells of rats treated with a specific combination of three chemicals had a longer lifecycle than untreated cells, you can't conclude that rats treated with the same combination of chemicals will live longer. You can't conclude this for a multitude of reasons, not the least of which is that cells behave differently when in a petri dish than when inside a living organism.

EXAMPLE OF HOW *NOT* TO WRITE YOUR CONCLUSIONS:

The results of this study suggest that men and women who qualified for the Olympic Marathon Trials trained differently.

EXAMPLE OF HOW TO WRITE YOUR CONCLUSIONS:

Men ran more than women for the year preceding the Olympic Trials. Both men and women performed the majority of their training slower than marathon pace. The amount of training performed at different intensities was similar between the sexes but included large variability as well. Among U.S. Olympic Marathon Trials qualifiers, no consensus exists as to how to prepare for the marathon beyond running at a pace slower than race pace.

Nearly half of men and nearly one-third of women did not have a coach, and two-thirds of the athletes trained alone. Between performance levels, it seems that the characteristics of training influence women's marathon performance more so than men's, as there were significant differences in average and peak training distance between elite and national-class women but not between elite and national-class men. In addition, women's marathon personal best time was correlated to the number of years of training, average weekly distance, peak weekly distance, and number of runs of at least 32 kilometers. Although data on the training characteristics of foreign long-distance runners are sparse, given what information is available, it seems that U.S. marathoners train less at higher intensities than foreign distance runners.

Further research should focus on the reasons these athletes trained the way they did. Particularly in the case of athletes who trained without a coach, the obvious question to be examined pertains to how these athletes obtained information on training. Also, the addition of physiological measurements to accompany the training characteristics of these athletes may offer deeper insight into the variables that influence marathon running performance.

In keeping with the formula of scientific dissertation writing, the following is a list of common phrases or sentences that you will read in other people's articles and dissertations, phrases that you should use often in your own writing:

- The results show that...
- Differences between our results and those of Smith et al. (2009) are due to methodological differences between studies. For example,...
- It is well known that...
- It is generally believed that...
- It has been known for a long time that...
- There is considerable evidence to support this finding.
- This finding is in agreement with the literature.
- It is unresolved that...
- For reasons not completely understood,...
- More research needs to be completed on...
- The data were analyzed using...
- These data are reported [listed] in Table 1.
- Figure 1 shows [illustrates, depicts]...
- It is possible that...
- The purpose of this study was to...

- It was hypothesized that…
- The main finding of this study was…
- An interesting finding of this study was…
- Smith et al. (2008) found that…
- Taken together, these findings suggest that…
- For example,…
- However,…
- In addition,…
- In summary,…
- In contrast, Smith and Jones (1998) found that…
- Each subject was verbally explained the procedures of the study and was required to sign an informed consent form.
- All procedures of this study were approved by the University of X's Human Subjects Committee.
- A one-way analysis of variance (ANOVA) was used to compare data between groups.
- There was a statistically significant difference between…
- In conclusion, the results of this study suggest that…
- Statistical significance was set at $p < 0.05$.
- X was significantly greater than Y.
- It has been suggested that…
- It has been found that…
- It has been reported that…
- It seems that…
- Previous studies have reported similar results.
- Further research should focus on…
- There is a scarcity of research focusing on…
- The research on X is equivocal.

More Advice on Writing Your Chapters

Since it took a long time to get my dissertation research off the ground, in part due to the time I spent waiting for my advisor to read my dissertation proposal and allow me to schedule my proposal defense, I began writing the Results and Discussion chapters of my dissertation before starting the research project in an attempt to save myself time on the back end of the research. Since my advisor told me that I should already know what my results should be based on my literature review–driven hypotheses before beginning the experiment, I wrote the Results and Discussion chapters assuming my hypotheses were correct. Even if some of my hypotheses were wrong, scientific language is easy to change. For example, it's easy to change a statement like "Treatment A had a significantly greater effect than treatment B" to "There was no significant difference in the effect of treatments A and B." At least I would have the template written before I even started the research, and I could just fill in the rest when the experiment was over.

However, like many of my ideas and attempts to get ahead, this idea blew up in my face, as I ended up pursuing a different dissertation topic with a different advisor. Writing twenty pages for your Results and Discussion chapters before your dissertation research begins only to change dissertation topics completely is yet another example of how not to earn your PhD degree.

Assuming you're not going to change your dissertation topic after writing your proposal, you may want to get a head start on the Results and Discussion chapters (or at least write an outline for them) while you wait to hear back from the Human Subjects Committee or your advisor about your proposal. This is a great way to feel productive during those inevitable periods of waiting.

If you have trouble writing any of your dissertation chapters, talk to your advisor and the other members of your committee. Make an appointment to meet with one or more of them to discuss specific issues you have. While the actual writing is solely your responsibility, feel free to discuss the technical aspects of your research, including ways to approach methodological issues with which you may be struggling as well as theories that may not be clear to you. Again, the members of the committee are there to help you, so take advantage of them. There will be times during graduate school when you'll be expected to stand on your own and run your own race, so to speak. Your advisor and your committee members cannot run the race for you, but they can (and should) prepare you to run that race successfully. After all, successful athletes don't train themselves—that's what a coach is for. If your dissertation is not going as well as you had planned—and whose does really?—don't get discouraged. Try to work through the rough patches, and seek the advice of your advisor and committee. Trust me, this is not the time to start thinking about changing your dissertation topic.

PROOFREAD

After you finish writing the first draft of your dissertation, proof-read it by reading the sentences out loud to yourself before you submit it to your advisor. For this, you may want to make sure your roommates are not home so you don't annoy or bore them to death. Remember, the dissertation is supposed to be scholarly work—submitting this work with spelling or grammatical mistakes are perfect examples of not successfully earning your PhD degree.

After submitting your dissertation to your advisor, celebrate by going out and partying with some friends. But don't party too hard because you don't want to be hungover when you have to get right back to work on the many revisions you'll have to make in order to satisfy your advisor and your committee. In response to once asking my advisor if he had ever told a student that the first draft of his or her proposal/dissertation was perfect, he told me that the big joke was that students used to hand him a red pen along with their manuscripts. I must have missed the punch line because I was not amused. The last thing I wanted to do was make revisions on what I thought was already perfect.

THE PROCRASTINATING ADVISOR

During the last few years of my degree, I spent more time waiting on other people than I spent actually working on my degree. The most difficult part of your PhD process may likely be the waiting, and the waiting for things over which you have no control, such as: advisor and committee reviews of your work, Human Subjects Committee and Institutional Review Board approvals, research assistants, among countless others. The list goes on and on. You're going to get frustrated. I did, and everyone I know who dealt with the same issues did. All you can do is learn to cope, get comfortable being a pest to the people on whom you rely, and try to come up with creative strategies to help move things along. I have a friend who received her PhD from the psychology department who told me all of the waiting during her PhD program has now affected her career as a university faculty member, as she makes sure that she is the first author on most of her papers so that she's always in control.

Of course, every once in a while, something will get done quickly. While my advisor took nearly four months to read and return my already-revised dissertation proposal only to tell me that it still wasn't good enough, my new dissertation advisor read my dissertation and gave me his feedback only one day after I had submitted the dissertation to him! I had to celebrate that success, obviously because what took my advisor one day took my committee a couple of months. One of my committee members actually took two months just to tell me she didn't like the style of the Introduction chapter within my dissertation proposal, even after it was approved by my dissertation advisor. Since the Introduction is the first chapter of the dissertation, it should have been the first part she read, and therefore, it should have taken her only a week to give me her feedback—unless, of course, the unread proposal sat on her desk for two months.

Throughout my degree, every time something was put back in my hands, I felt like I had to rush to complete the work, to compensate for the slowness of others, to make up for what I perceived as lost time. As a result, all I did was hurry up and wait for the latter half of my degree. This created an unnecessary and stressful situation. Rushing to get your work done in an attempt to make up for lost time is yet another example of how not to earn your PhD degree.

Because professors don't have deadlines to complete their work (as many other professionals outside of academia do), they often take a long time to finish things. Some professors don't have this problem—they're great at setting deadlines for themselves—but others are, quite frankly, procrastinators. Don't accept long waits from your advisor or committee members to read and review your submitted work. Remind them nicely that the timeframe of your degree depends on them. The student's educational process should not be slowed down randomly; it must remain a high priority for your advisor and your committee. If your advisor does not give you feedback in a timely manner, talk to your department chairperson or a dean. If that doesn't resolve the issue, you may have to change your advisor. I ended up doing just that, and it turned out to be the right decision. This may sound harsh, but you cannot complete a PhD program without your advisor's cooperation. After all, that's what he or she is getting paid to do—help you.

As long as you pay tuition to the university, your advisor works for you—even if you have an assistantship and have your tuition waived, your advisor still works for you. Unfortunately, too many advisors don't see it that way. My advisor saw his students as his subordinates. Like all of his students, I was expected to wait on his approval and permission to take each step forward, even when I was the lead researcher on a project and the first author on the resulting manuscript. My advisor wouldn't even let me submit my dissertation proposal to the other members of my committee until he had read my revisions and was satisfied with the pages. However, months would pass without him reading and providing feedback on my proposal.

The dissertation process, as I was told by my department chairperson at the time, is not supposed to be a back-and-forth affair solely between student and advisor, only submitting your work to your committee after the advisor has approved it. You should feel free to share your proposal with your other committee members and ask for their feedback, too. If your advisor doesn't like you doing this, then he or she is not the right advisor for you. If you have a good advisor, he or she will not only tell you how to make your dissertation better; instead, he or she will show you how to please the other members of the committee.

PREPARING YOUR DISSERTATION PROPOSAL PRESENTATION

When you've completed your proposal and your dissertation, the next step is to create a presentation for your formal discussion in front of your committee. Since all your committee members will have read (or should have read) your proposal (and subsequent dissertation) before your presentation, your presentation should simply be an overview of your proposed research. In the old days, people used real slides, loading them into a carousel on a slide projector. Things have become much easier and quicker now. Most students use computer slide presentation programs like Microsoft PowerPoint and integrate a laptop computer with an LCD projector that displays the images on a screen to show the presentation.

To create your presentation, simply copy and paste text from your proposal or dissertation into your PowerPoint slides. Remember, there's no reason to reinvent the wheel. Here are some things to keep in mind when preparing your presentation:

- As with your written proposal and dissertation, make sure you don't have any spelling or grammatical mistakes.

- Use a large font size so everyone in the room can read it.
- Don't crowd your slides by putting too many words on each.
- Use color for emphasis, especially on graphs.
- Remember, a picture says a thousand words. Show the picture. Speak the words.
- Don't use red text on a black or blue background, or any other combination of text and background color that is not easy on the eyes.
- Be thorough, but don't be wordy. Not every word in your written proposal or dissertation needs to be included in your presentation. Use keywords and phrases rather than whole sentences and paragraphs.
- Put your purpose statement and hypotheses on separate slides so they stand out.
- Ask your advisor how much time you will be given for your presentation, and then plan accordingly.

The presentation should follow the same format as your proposal, including Introduction, Purpose, Hypotheses, Literature Review, Methodology, and Limitations sections—the dissertation defense presentation will contain the added sections Results, Discussion, and Conclusions. For nonscientific disciplines, your presentation will be much different and can take on a number of formats. But regardless of what discipline you're pursuing, there will almost always be an introduction, some kind of statement of the problem or thesis statement, and how you plan on approaching the problem or supporting your thesis by extension.

After you have finished creating your presentation, rehearse for your proposal defense. You don't want to go into the conference room cold. If you can, rehearse in front of other people. When you rehearse the presentation, use the same laptop computer and projector you will use for the real thing, and go through your show in its entirety. Changing computers for the presentation often changes the formatting of the slides unless you use the same type of computer and the same version of PowerPoint. The more you have rehearsed your presentation beforehand, the easier and better it will be when you stand in front of your committee and do it for real.

THE DISSERTATION PROPOSAL DEFENSE

The dissertation proposal defense (sometimes called a meeting) is scheduled after all of your committee members have read your proposal. It's a formal look at the proposal and your proposed research, during which potential problems can be addressed and resolved. For scientific disciplines, the proposal defense is straightforward because you basically reiterate what you've already written in your proposal. You have to explain your study to your committee, outline your hypotheses, and explain your methods. For nonscientific disciplines, it's much different. You typically have to lay out the "problem" you'll discuss in your dissertation and the theoretical groundwork for your analysis, discuss the questions and challenges you might expect, and justify what you're including and excluding to your committee.

Since you will likely discuss your research with your advisor many times before your proposal meeting and revise your proposal a few times based on his or her feedback, the proposal meeting with the entire committee should be not much more than a formality. However, getting four or five people to agree on anything is difficult, so even if your advisor approves the research and is content with your approach, your committee members may still have issues.

In fact, after my advisor approved my research, a couple of my other committee members still requested revisions to my proposal before they agreed to schedule a meeting with me. It's possible that your committee members will not read your proposal before the meeting, instead choosing to wait until you present it to them. At the meeting, if the committee deems that there are many revisions necessary, they may request a second proposal meeting. More commonly, however, if any revisions are warranted, the committee will approve the proposal on the terms that you make the revisions before continuing forward.

Your proposal defense is a publicly announced affair that is open to the university community; however, only your committee members can ask you questions. Anyone else in the room can only sit and listen. It may help to invite some friends to make you feel more at ease—just make sure they don't make funny faces at you from the back of the room.

Remember that it's your committee's job to ask you to defend your decisions. It's a learning process during which your committee may make suggestions regarding how to address the proposed problem. Your committee wants to see that you have seriously thought about your research project and how it fits into the bigger picture of your discipline. That said, here are some questions you should be prepared to answer during your proposal defense:

- How can the results of your proposed research be applied?
- Why did you choose that particular study design?
- Why did you choose to measure those particular variables?
- How did you decide on the number of subjects? (The correct answer to this is that you did a power analysis using effect sizes from the literature or your own pilot study data. The wrong answer to this is that it was your lucky number.)

- How much power does your study have?
- How much of an effect do you expect to see?
- What are your expected results?
- What are the rationales for your hypotheses?
- What types of statistical procedures will you use? What statistic is suited for each hypothesis?
- If you don't expect to find a statistically significant difference between treatments or testing conditions in one of your measured variables, is that variable still worth measuring?
- How much variability in your data do you expect to see?
- What are your inclusion and exclusion criteria for subject selection? How have you controlled for those criteria?
- What are your study's limitations?
- How do you plan to handle this problem (if one exists)? Statistically? Experimentally?
- What are your reasons for doing this research? What question(s) do you hope to answer?
- What is evident from past research?
- What new thing or idea does your research contribute to the literature?

SO WHAT?

After explaining my proposed study to my committee during my proposal meeting, one of my committee members asked me, "So what?" Talk about a question to take the wind out of your sails! After trying to explain my reasons for doing the research and what it would contribute to the literature, that same committee member actually said to me, in front of the rest of my committee no less, "I don't think this research is sophisticated enough for a doctoral dissertation. It's more like a good master's thesis." Ouch! At the time, besides being embarrassed, I felt that comment was misdirected, especially since the research was my advisor's idea! This is not a good thing to hear because you don't want to spend all of your time and energy changing your proposed research project to satisfy one committee member or convince that committee member that what you already have is indeed sophisticated enough for a PhD dissertation. Needless to say, that committee member was promptly removed from my committee and replaced by someone else. To prevent the "So what?" question from being asked of you, make sure you know exactly why you are doing the proposed research and what that research will contribute to the literature.

THE DISSERTATION DEFENSE

After you have completed your dissertation research, written the remaining chapters of your dissertation, and revised them based on comments from your advisor and committee members, you will then set a date to stand before your committee once more, this time to defend your dissertation.

Check with the university graduate school about setting a defense date, as the timelines vary between schools. At my university, the dissertation defense date had to be scheduled at least thirty days in advance of the defense. Also, check that everything else is in order, such as having the required number of credits for graduation,

Human Subjects Committee or other Institutional Review Board approval of your research, and approval for the nomination of your research committee, which should be approved before you begin your research. You don't want to find out that a form has not been filed by the appropriate committee or the university graduate school at the last minute. Unfortunately, there are forms that must be filed throughout your degree, some of which have timelines associated with them; and it's extremely easy for those forms to be misplaced, especially when dealing with more than one person. Being told two weeks before your dissertation defense that your research committee has not been approved by the university graduate school is yet another example of how not to earn your PhD degree.

When everything is in place and your defense date and room have been set, you (or your committee chair) will submit your dissertation abstract, signed by your committee chair, to the university graduate school so that your defense can be formally announced to the university community. This is when the fun begins. Unless you're so proud of your dissertation and so extremely confident that your defense will go off without a hitch, you probably don't want other graduate students or faculty other than your committee members to be present. Unfortunately, this isn't your choice, as dissertation defenses are open to the university community.

A TALE OF TWO CITIES

My dissertation defense was a bit unorthodox, primarily because I had completed my dissertation research and worked with an advisor at a university other than the one from which I would be receiving my degree. After I completed my dissertation and my defense was set, both my dissertation advisor and I flew across the country to my former university to defend my dissertation in front of the rest of my committee, which certainly added a lot of drama to an already dramatic event.

Having to arrange for my dissertation defense from across the country, I had to rely on my committee co-chair at the university of the defense location to sign and submit the defense announcement. After he did this, I found out that the room that was chosen for my defense was right next door to my old advisor's office! Given our history, he was the one person I did *not* want in attendance. Changing advisors and then having your dissertation defense next door to your old advisor's office is another example of how not to successfully earn your PhD degree. Even though dissertation defenses are open to the university community, if you feel uncomfortable with a specific person in attendance, you can respectfully ask that person not to attend. It is *your* day, after all. Thankfully, my old advisor did not attend my dissertation defense.

As the last obstacle standing between you and your degree, the dissertation defense has more expectations associated with it than the proposal defense. It's treated like an exam as a result. Unlike the proposal defense, which is more of a collaborative discussion of your proposed work, during which time your committee members may suggest changes or ideas for you to incorporate into your project, the dissertation defense is just that—a defense of your scholarly work. It's your final exam and your final performance. You either pass, or you fail. It's the defining moment of your PhD program. In short, it's a very big deal, and everyone knows it. You can always tell when there's a dissertation defense happening. You can hear the whispers of people in the hallway as they pass by the room: "There's a dissertation defense going on in there." The importance of the moment is palpable.

Depending on the philosophy of your department and your committee members, you may or may not be given any feedback on your dissertation before your defense. While my dissertation advisor was very open with his students, discussing their dissertations at length with them so the defense was not much more than a formality, my committee members at the university from which I was obtaining my degree were much stricter with their process. Although they had my dissertation in their hands three and a half months before my defense, not one of them provided any feedback before the defense, despite mine and my advisor's requests. As a result, I had no idea what they thought about my dissertation going into my defense, and I certainly didn't know what they were going to ask. I felt like they weren't showing me their cards, like I was being set up to fail, especially given my history with my committee members.

While I expected to make revisions on the dissertation before the defense, it didn't happen that way at all. I wasn't sure whether their lack of feedback was merely an oversight on their part, a purposeful action, or the faculty's philosophy that doctoral candidates are expected to stand on their own. It may very well have been the latter. A student I knew in the psychology department had the same experience. "My advisor and committee members did not prep me for likely questions," she said. "I was expected to be able to think on my feet. Basically, I had to be able to tear my study apart better than any of them! I was even expected to know things beyond what I had written about in my dissertation."

When you submit your dissertation to your committee members, ask them if and when they will provide feedback. You may even want to find out from the university graduate school if committees are required to provide feedback to students before their defenses. Regardless of whether or not your committee provides feedback and requires revisions before the defense, expect that you will have at least some revisions to make afterward.

Much like the qualifying exam, the committee is both your opposing attorneys and your jury at the defense. But you shouldn't worry—because you're prepared, or at least you will be. Since student dissertation defenses are open to other students and faculty, sit in on the defenses of other students. Better yet, attend the defenses of other students who have at least one of the same committee members as you. You will gain valuable knowledge of what to expect, including what types of questions are asked, how the committee members act, and how the successful (and unsuccessful) students act. I never sat in on any defenses, and that was a mistake. The more you can learn about the process and demystify it, the better off you'll be come defense day.

As you prepare for your dissertation defense, try to anticipate the questions that your committee may ask. Your questions will likely be content-specific. Are there obvious places in your dissertation where a committee member could easily attack you? You probably won't get any "How will this affect the world?" types of questions, but below are listed some questions you should be prepared to answer during your dissertation defense:

- Can you clearly summarize your important findings?
- What would you do to follow up on specific problems and findings?
- What is new and important in your dissertation? What does this research contribute to the current body of literature?

- Can you explain your ideas in this section?
- Is there another way, experimentally or statistically, you could have tested your hypotheses?
- Were there any confounding variables?
- How confident are you that your results are valid? What evidence do you have?
- How can this research be extended? What steps should be taken next?
- What are the implications of your research?
- Why do you think you didn't find what you thought you were going to find? Why do you think your hypotheses were wrong?
- And my favorite…what have you done that merits a PhD?

Since you have already defended your proposal well before you've reached your dissertation defense, your committee should not ask you to defend your methodology or your approach. If they have any problems with your proposal, those should have been addressed a long time ago. The dissertation defense is not the time to have to redefend how you did your study or how you approached your topic. That would be like just finishing building a house only to be asked why you built it the way you did. You should be asked about your blueprint before you plan to build the house. Some may think it's completely fair to ask such questions after the fact, but that's the purpose of the proposal defense, not the dissertation defense. What you should be asked to defend during your dissertation defense are your results, not your research plan. Usually the committee knows something about the subject and other research in that area, so they'll undoubtedly try to trip you up. You need to defend your research while thinking clearly but without being defensive in style. Being clear and concise are assets.

While your committee members shouldn't question your intentions after all the work you've completed, we all do things from time to time that we shouldn't. Since the methodology of scientific studies is a big part of doing scientific research, you should still prepare to defend the choices you made concerning the methods you employed because they'll likely come up again. Critique your own methods before your committee does. While you cannot control the choices of your committee members regarding their questions, you can control your own choices; and the dissertation defense is not the time to make bad choices. Here are some things you should *not* do at your dissertation defense:

- Ask your committee members to hold hands, and start the meeting off with a prayer.
- Give a sixty-minute presentation when you've been asked to speak for only thirty minutes.
- Give a ten-minute presentation when you've been asked to speak for a whole thirty minutes.
- Ask your committee members to stand at the beginning of your defense and face the flag while you sing the National Anthem.
- Answer every question with a question.
- Say "Umm…" at the beginning of every sentence.
- Tell your friends who attend your defense to clap and whistle at the end of your presentation.
- Exclaim "*Voila!*" when you present your results.
- Say "I'd like to introduce my friend, Joe, who will now explain the next part of this dissertation."
- Say "I didn't know I was supposed to know that."
- Dress in a T-shirt and jeans.
- Pace back and forth around the room.
- Have a cover charge at the door.

- Sell raffle tickets to the attendees.
- Hire a clown to stand in the corner of the room and make balloon animals.
- Serve popcorn.
- Say to a committee member, "That's a stupid question."
- Argue with your committee members.

On the day of your presentation, get to the room early so you have time to set up the equipment and make sure everything is working. When you speak, look your committee members in the eyes. Don't be timid; but don't be cocky either. Be confident and act like the expert your committee is expecting you to be. This confidence comes from being prepared, so study all of the aspects of your dissertation for your presentation and practice the presentation until you can recite it by heart.

When the members of your committee ask you questions, take your time to formulate a response. Remember that you are in control. You should never feel rushed. Often, they will ask questions because they don't know the answers themselves and hope that you can educate them. This may sound backwards, but that's what makes the dissertation defense unique—you are the expert rather than your committee members. Saying "That's a good question, Dr. Nobel" will flatter the committee member and may make him or her more likely to take your side. Remember, your committee wants you to pass, and it's a lot more complicated for them to fail you than to pass you, after all. They are simply giving you the opportunity to show that you understand your research, can add to the body of knowledge in your research area, and can stand on your own two feet as a scholar. They want to see that you can speak clearly about what you've done. Is that so much to ask?

When your committee is done asking you questions, you will then be asked to leave the room while the committee members deliberate. If they agree that you have passed, they will sign the acceptance page of your dissertation. It doesn't matter by how small of a margin you pass, just as long as you pass. No one—except maybe your family—will ever ask you. You may have heard the old joke often told to medical students: "What do you call someone who graduated last in medical school?" the answer being "Doctor." So what do you call someone who barely passes his or her dissertation defense? "Doctor" is what you call them. Remember, the best dissertation is one that is signed by your committee members, since their signatures mean that you have passed your dissertation defense. Once the degree is done, it doesn't matter so much exactly when or how you got it or even how the defense went, because you have your PhD now.

YOU GET DONE WHEN YOU GET DONE

When your committee signs that most important acceptance page of your dissertation, you can finally breathe a big sigh of relief. Feel free to hug your committee members. And pop open the champagne—congratulations are in order. You've obtained the prestigious PhD degree. You have become a member of the exclusive club. But wait! You'll still likely have revisions to make before submitting your dissertation to the university graduate school, so the sooner you get them done, the sooner you can really celebrate. Once all your revisions are made, have a few copies of your dissertation bound—one for you, one for your department and/or advisor, and one for your parents (and anyone else you want). It may be a bit expensive, but it's worth the money. After all, you only get one PhD. Unless you're a bit crazy, that is, and decide to go for another one after this grueling process. In fact, I knew one student in my department who obtained a PhD in zoology and then started working on his second PhD in biomechanics! Now that's crazy!

So revel in the glory. And as my twin brother would tell you, you are now a "*Ph*ony *D*octor" for the rest of your life. If you're like me at all, you wouldn't want it any other way.

Epilogue

Despite what people think when they find out that I have a PhD to my credit, school never came easy to me. When I was young, little did I (or anyone else) know that I would one day earn my PhD degree—certainly not my kindergarten teacher, who scolded me for pushing one of my classmates against the cubbies because he broke my Batman action figure, causing the poor kid a head injury that required stitches; certainly not my middle school French teacher, who kept yelling out my American name with a French accent in the middle of class as I clowned around; certainly not the substitute teachers in high school, who tried to give me detention after I threw paper airplanes across the classroom, sometimes landing them on the teacher's desk; and certainly not my twin brother, who has always rightfully thought of himself as the smarter one, even after all these years. Maybe my sixth grade math teacher had a hint of what was to come as she told my mother during a parent-teacher conference that I was "a wiz at math," or maybe she was just trying to find something positive to say.

Both my father, who passed away when I was eight years old, and my mother would have had every reason to believe that between their twin sons, Jack would be the one more likely to earn a PhD. After all, he was the one who spent weeks in first grade researching and preparing a slideshow on dinosaurs and exhausting our parents by studying every single display in New York's Museum of Natural History; he was the one who helped the neighbor's kid make an active volcano for his class science project; and he was the one who would later go on to spend his first year and a half in college on the dean's list majoring in aerospace engineering before getting even better grades with a double major in psychology and English. But even if I weren't the likely candidate back then, I know that my father, who never attended college himself, probably would have been both bewildered by the fact that someone would want to spend so many years in school and immensely proud of his son for the accomplishment. I know my mother is, mostly because she tells me this every day.

Being smart is just one part—maybe even a small one at that—of earning a PhD degree. The larger, more important part is making the right choices, being persistent, and understanding how to work the system and the process. That's the true secret of how to survive and conquer the PhD process.

While the PhD process is a stressful undertaking, much of that stress can be avoided if you choose your advisor carefully. That is why Chapter 1 is the most important chapter of this book—it sets the stage for everything else to come. In this book, I have tried to give you the kind of advice that I myself could have used before I went through the PhD process. Now it's up to you to follow the advice and earn your own PhD degree. When you do, I want to hear about it.

At university graduations, it's customary for the president of the university to state the new responsibility that accompanies the degree when conferring them upon graduates. This responsibility couldn't be more present than with a doctoral degree. It's only the highest academic degree you can receive, after all. Whatever path you take after graduation, remember that responsibility, and remember how hard you worked for it.

I've met many people with master's degrees or bachelor's degrees in my discipline who act as if they have PhDs. They think they have tons of knowledge. They go around referring to themselves as physiologists. They think a graduate degree is a graduate degree. Sometimes, if they can, they cite the literature, thinking that impresses others. But as I learned over the seven years while going through the process, there is a huge difference between a master's degree and a PhD. This difference is definitely larger than between a bachelor's degree and a master's degree. There's the obvious time difference—since it takes only two years to obtain a master's degree while it requires at least four years (and often more) to obtain a PhD—but time is only the minor difference. There is a large transformation that takes place over the time between your master's degree and your PhD. You go from reading the research of others to being one of the researchers yourself. You go from reading the works of other scholars to being one of the scholars whose work is read. You go from reading the novels of others to writing your own novels. You go from being on the outside looking in to being on the inside looking out. You go from watching the poker game to sitting at the table with your own set of chips. You attend conferences to present your research, no longer as a graduate student, but as a member of the academic professorate. Despite all the stress, frustration, and anxiety that accompanies the pursuit of a PhD degree, that's pretty darn cool.

About the Author

Jason R. Karp, PhD, received his PhD in exercise physiology in 2007 after seven years of doctoral work, during which he learned everything you shouldn't do if you want to have a PhD in four years. He is a prolific freelance writer, professional running coach, and owner of RunCoachJason.com. Jason R. Karp has also written *Directions for SPSS®: A Manual for Students in Statistics* (Bloomington, IN: RunCoachJason.com, 2004).